changing
the
family

changing
the
family

Warren M. Brodey, M. D.

Clarkson N. Potter, Inc./Publisher

NEW YORK

THE PARTS

acknowledgments

Many people are imaged in this book and I am grateful for each refreshing experience they provided. Edward T. Hall, Marshall McLuhan, Warren McCulloch; Marvin Minski, Gordon Pask, Peter Oser, Avery Johnson, Jim Bever, Sam Mason, Bob and Marge Kvarnes, Robert Cohen, William Malamud, Ali Javan, Nathan Ackerman, Bernard Bandler, Eleanor Ring, Anna Freud, Phyllis Noble, Oliver Selfridge, Kevin Lynch, Frank Fremont-Smith, Eugene Bell, Betty Basamania, Bob Dysinger, Murray Bowen, George Gardner, Frieda Fromm Reichmann, John Murray, Uno Helgeson, Seymour Papert, Ruth Burr, Winifred Whitman, Anders Richter, Myron Colers, Harold Hughes, Don Jackson, Buckminster Fuller, Gregory Bateson, Norbert Weiner, Alfred Korzybski, E. E. Cummings, Gertrude Stein, Eugène Ionesco, Samuel Beckett, Jerry Lettvin, Jean and Frank Getlein, Martin Shubik, and George DeVincent— this is but a short list of those who have had, directly or indirectly, the kind of impact that one uses to evolve this kind of book.

Many families, too, have shown me their stories, that I might understand their styles and learn better to be able to communicate technically, as well as personally, their ways of changing. My own family has grown through these involvements. No single family is represented by any one of the stories I have told.

Among the many institutions that have helped me on my way are the National Aeronautic and Space Agency, the Washington School of Psychiatry, the Washington Psychoanalytic Institute, Massachusetts Institute of Technology, the Office of Economic Opportunity, the National Institutes of Mental Health, the Creative Science Seminar of New York University, the Human Ecology Fund, the Pilot School for Blind Children, and the Environmental Ecology Laboratory.

I am especially indebted to Clarkson Potter, to his editor Jane West, to Dimmes Bishop, and Douglas Brown of the United Kingdom for making this manuscript available to the readers.

A family is a living
thing,
A creature
spanning time

husband and wife

A HUSBAND AND WIFE in contact speak a million million words in every breath. It is this richness that encompasses a family into a living unit and carries on its life into an evolving generation. Yes, the contact I speak of is not of love or of hate but of both, and it includes all the formal words that are used to label the embodiments of living. But the embodiments of living are beyond the words we use. A child is born into the livingness or deadness of a family and is joined by his moment-to-moment learning to the family way of evolution.

A child and a mother and a father may live in a flatland of photograph-like words amid the shadows in the cave or be penetrated by the sun's warming rays. It is not the warmth of the sun that I speak of, but the knowledge of the seasons, the snow, ice, water, heat, and changings in one another's way of life, which even as they evolve to adapt to internal and external evolutions, grow in a way that is more or less adaptive. Darwin, when he spoke of adaptation to reality as a means of survival, spoke not of happiness or sadness, anger or hate, but rather of the need to act in response to what exists—and to know and learn in this sense the system of evolving that we transmit across the generations and through the ages of our species. Yes, the capacity to evolve is learned.

A wife and her husband are two different creatures in a fundamental way, but their union creates from this difference not only the child of their delight but also the freshening capacity to unify their sense of variation into a combination that has more evolving power than each alone.

And each senses the other's reality and changes as the other changes, performing the filigreed dance of life, always changing though inevitably repeating in a new way the age-old dance, which holds its character by changing to meet the requirements of aging. Each growth makes the old behavior new because it has a different context. This is the concept of a psychology that does not deny time.

This kind of contact is not to be confused with just touching or holding on. Nor is it to be confounded with being good or evil, creative or destructive. What I refer to is more basic. Contact contains the species evolution within the unit, family. Society evolves and so do cells, and each to prevent its extinction must recognize its environment in an action way that adapts for survival. The family unit, like a person, regenerates itself—it has a life. And man and woman sense each other's changing and maintain their contact, being responsive to each new moment of their contact.

A million million bits of learning about their way of being a living unit happen every moment. But some families do not live in this rich bath of changing with environmental information. Their eyes are closed by a logic of words untempered by their breathing. And such husbands and wives cannot even fight except for a momentary tearing to reach through emptiness. More often this emptiness is unknown—brought up without contact—unknown to the rich fullness of arms hugging hugged and changing in the moment as each feels each other's changings and welcomes the discovery of each other's evolving newness. But I am not speaking of happiness or sadness, for newness may be sad and deadly but not deadening in the sense of robbing vigor.

Yes, there are those who live a more dead way of life and do not engage in the contact of knowing, even intuitively, that there is a world that they deny because for now it is too painful and there is no use in being aware.

I am not speaking in favor of great gushings of information back and forth or hand holdings or honesty or such like slogans. Information exchange is evolution and evolution is the human business.

A child who is not taught how to evolve will die even if he remains stick-and-bones alive.

A million million learnings are in the timing of each person's changing with each other's contrapuntal changings, and this is easier to think of in music than in the language of who-done-what-to-whom, which does not flow as music —each note's meaning changing with its timing and with its relation to others of its family.

Good music has its themes that repeat with a variation resonant in the changing environment of other notes. And a husband who does not change with his wife's menstrual period is fooled if he thinks that his language is the same even when his words are no different—the context is changed. And the language of changing with each other's change is a million times richer than who said what to whom. It is this richness that allows us to train the animal child into a human—a very complex skill that we humans have developed over time.

And I don't mean that contact is joy. It can be misery. But it is real—even real enough sometimes to know that only fantasy derived from inside can allow one to persist when all logic says there is no way. The logic we have is limited by the human capacity to conceive. And each person and the child teach one another in the way they move and smell and touch the aspects of one another that, before, were beyond even the slightest sense that there was pattern. Contact joins a family in metabolizing what was beyond knowing into the exquisite first glimmer of pattern. And this is the beginning of a husband and wife learning to teach each other of each other's worlds that cannot be experienced directly. It is this teaching that allows a family to work at adapting for survival in a way that transcends their separate ways of life and brings an informational union that has advantage for survival.

And this that I speak of has little to do with legal doctrines except that doctrines survive because they have been at one time a convenience that made unnecessary the working over of the same issue. Doctrine can become a group of words which, by conveniently labeling a relationship, denies that relationship's self-regenerating richness—a richness that creates something quite beyond the list of all its names. Yes, a family is more than the sum of its people and its names, and contact is what makes it that way. . . .

And contact can occur beyond all family limits. It is a

kind of stabilizing that encompasses change, but in a way that maintains the boundaries of change within limits that are commensurate with living. But contact has another function. It enables two creatures to produce by their union a set of others who are different in a way that extends the boundaries within which the species can exist ever so slightly in the direction necessary to survival. Contact is the means of behavioral evolution and is symmetrical with the process of species-evolution that Darwin describes.

Death and extinction come to those who cannot evolve. Obsolescence of a marriage is a kind of death that is familiar. Contact allows the family to die and be reborn with each learning, changing *what was* to *what is more viable* in the new context.

And the senescence of a couple who died long ago or when their children left may represent their incapacity to change their action toward each other when the kind of action possible was changed.

Some families do not survive the changing ecology of a the new context.

Contact is a direction of evolving. Out-of-contact is a kind of decay that can occur when the pores are not open, when senses being dulled become less aware of what is to be sensed and become more dull. Here, I remind you that I am not talking of the value of being more open. Being closed, being unaware, being insensitive, unresponsive—even dying for the moment—may be a part of staying alive. A mother who does not learn to turn off her radar at just the right time may prevent her child's creating a world that has his uniqueness contained in the way *he* arranges its contact with his reality. This fullness the mother can never know, having been brought up in a different time with a different set of parents. And the toys and teddy bears arrange themselves to understand.

Time moves forward never to be repeated even as a husband and wife reminisce together about times very differently conceived in the light of subsequent events. And even in talking of the past, their way of talking speaks of their movement forward as they curl and twine together.

And it is my purpose in this book to point out the difference between the hand held like wood and the myriad impulses and learnings and teachings and information exchanges and breathings that teach and learn a million million lessons within a single breath. And this is the way we join in evolving each other. Two people glancing into each other's eyes change each other's way of looking by the way that each looks. Two hands holding speak moment to moment. These messages give substance to our evolution. They begin the groupings, they induce the exchanging awareness of patterns that allow us to know enough to survive. Even as I expect your hand to receive mine, I speak and you add a slight movement and I change the voice in my hand to reach the you whom I did not expect. And you change to meet the new word of tone and rhythm. And we both change together until the changing becomes a language much richer than the literal meaning of the words. Then you begin to know contact as a mutual commitment to evolving ourselves and each other and them.

The stories that follow grow out of many. They are little descriptions of families mixed with just enough comment and contrast to tell their own story and insist that you listen and feel and sometimes get sick and feel funny and a little disorganized until it all pops together when you have heard it repeating. Then you know something new, which may not have words yet. But then the same situation hits *you*, and you *act* someway differently because the new way you now know about occurs to you.

beginning impression

THE TELEPHONE RINGS. "I'm calling," Mother says, "because school told me my son needs help, and they gave me your name."

Silence.

"Could you tell me briefly about the problem, Mrs. Moran?"

She continues: "My child has a short span of attention. He is not doing well in school, though he is said to be intelligent. My husband and I want him to have all the breaks. He is in private school now. He went through public school making straight C's. He wasn't up with his class. He likes toys, and, oh, he's worried that he won't live through the Christmas season."

My ears are flapping. Mother's voice is soft and steady and concerned. It has no cutting edge, nor is it helpless. There is no expectation of miracles. This will be an easy one, I think. I have an hour and would like to see the whole family. She replies, "That's fine. We're all worried, and we know we're part of the trouble. Fred and his older sister fight all the time. Their both coming should help that." The appointment is set.

Usually it is Mother who calls, sometimes Father, sometimes the referring physician, the school, or the social agency. There are many calls and many questions. The family therapist has many techniques of responding.

"Should we bring the baby?" "Yes, by all means." "Which children should we leave at home?" "None." "Why the baby?" "Is the problem any different since the baby came?" "Well, my son is jealous, but then all children are. At school he does seem younger than his age. He wants to be put back a grade, the teacher says." "Well, bring the baby and your husband and your son and daughter and we'll see what we can work out together."

"He's working," the mother replies. "Well, I can see you only if your husband is interested in coming." "He's not interested," she answers. "He's this boy's stepfather." She begins to cry. "I thought it would be so different.

"He yells at the boy—I feel so hurt," the mother adds.

"The first hour may be like home" is my wry answer to her concern that if she really asks the stepfather to come he may say embarrassing and nasty things. "But that's the problem we will work at."

To see this mother and her child without new siblings and without the stepfather's presence is to treat a family now defunct. If I unintentionally aid and abet the alienation of a stepfather, I slow the integration of a family.

Is the child of the first marriage, out of supposed loyalty to dear old seductive Dad, who drank and gave presents, keeping Mother and her new husband apart? Mother's guilt, Father's newness, some jealousy . . . a new family is being formed—these are thoughts at my end of the telephone as I listen to more detail. To bring in the action-father is to realize the conflict. This is faster than talking about it.

A mother begins her call with "What do you think, should we tell little Billy that he is going to see a psychiatrist? He has always been a good boy and now he talks back. We know there is something wrong with him or he'd love his mother." Mother awaits my answer. She has read what I am supposed to reply.

"Uh huh," I answer, while I think of what to say.

"Well, maybe it's a family problem and Billy is just a part, but he does need help," his mother answers, waiting.

Pushed, I unhappily reply: "Why don't you tell him that you are all unhappy, and you are going to see a psychiatrist who will help the family feel better?"

She replies: "My husband does think he's more of a boy now. I sometimes think I did protect him too much." Pause. She awaits my chastising lecture over the telephone.

I delay, then respond. "We'll talk it over next Wednesday." My voice drops to end the call.

She continues: "Do you think my son should be told that the teacher thinks he is not doing well at school, even though he is bright? We'll come to see you but if you mention *that,* it will hurt his self-esteem. . . ."

And so it goes. The telephone calls are always fascinating. There are the words, the tone of voice, the rhythm, the edge of tension, the wail of tears, the breathing or the heavy breathing. There is my own reaction, too—the sense of concern, anger at being tricked, the helpless panic that makes me helpless too.

The first telephone contacts set an image astir. Is the father brought into the conversation as if he had no meaning? Has the child been consulted? Is Mother affirming that he wants to come? Is it that the child's nightmares keep Father awake? Or is it the child's dream of falling through space—the content of the nightmare—that Mother is concerned about?

Father telephones. He says the boy's mother has been ill. She has had a nervous breakdown. "My son seems anxious all the time. He wants to win as if to prove himself: he worries so much about winning that it worries me. I don't think he'll ever be a success. He does not know about his mother's illness—he must respect her." Father's voice is soft, controlled. I answer, "When you come, bring Mother too. She will want to help."

Each family handles its telephone call differently. Who calls is important. So is the role set for the doctor. Long apologies and high respect may mean a lower-class orientation. "They told me I'd have to call" is not likely to come from a middle-class family; there, controlling one's own destiny is so important. Similarly, "Dr. So-and-So gave me your name" and a mild compliment smooth the way for upper-class operations. The lower-class family that calls a psychiatrist for consultation without being sent has attributes that will be interesting to explore.

For the skilled listener, the telephone conversation begins the focusing of communication process. Sometimes he hears what sounds like recital—complaints against some other person or a precise listing of "symptoms." He hears but does not necessarily accept the family's "diagnosis" of, for example, who is "the sick one" and in need of help. Merely accepting the communication of the family's way of diagnosing illness and allowing this to determine who is to be seen would deny the total family involvement.

The therapist uses the telephone call to begin evaluation of the family's pressure toward making the as yet unknown doctor conform to an expected and traditional family role. Even over the telephone, some families expect judgment, chastisement, or praise. The specific nature of the pressure, like the family's diagnosis, may be another symptom.

In the telephone call the therapist must not unwittingly accept the role pressure. But he must be wary of how his effort to hold position is communicating. Whatever he says will be deciphered and reported by the caller. After he has been filtered through the anticipation background of the family member when he sat down to dial, he may be heard as fitting the role pressure. Certain family telephones have their own restrictive sending and receiving systems.

Once all the family members sit together in the family therapy situation, they can compare and contrast their appraisal of a common reality; each can have confidence in his own appraisal. But when one family member is sole interpreter of the outside to the others, the opportunity for distortion is enhanced. An intrinsic part of the family's problem may be the distortion of what one does not say. Questions that the doctor did not ask are carried to the family as the significant response. What to me is but ten moments to answer messages between appointments may answer long hours of bated breath or screamings.

One listens and speaks from the beginning so as to approach the family.

"Jimmy is stuttering," she says.

"And how is the whole family communicating?"

"His father used to stutter" or "We don't talk much" or "Everyone goes his own way" will *not* be obtained by responding to the mother's chief complaint by asking the apparently neutral question: "And how long has he been stuttering?" This is not to say that one does not wish to know the duration of Jimmy's stuttering problem. Rather, one has selected a response from the multitude of possible responses in terms of therapeutic direction that relates to the family unit. Then, later, when you watch the stuttering son interrupted in the middle of a breath or accused of merely making a noise, the whole situation and its problem are differently perceived, and a new set of responses is engendered.

One listens on the telephone to discover the ear-mouth loop—the listening with the ears and speaking with the mouth sound exchange and timing system. Then, during a therapy hour, the nineteen-year-old sister, in town for Easter vacation, describes the family when the boy at two years old began to speak.

"His beginning baby talk was called stuttering," she accuses, "but they knew he'd have trouble just like Daddy does," she sneers. "They did it to me too, and I still get even by murdering the language—and Father corrects me."

A family's communication of *its* diagnosis can bring about the symptoms: the driver stiff from fear of skidding is a likely victim at the next curve.

An unskilled listener may bring a child closer to the firing line. The boy had had a medical treatment—his mother called it—because he wouldn't hear—or couldn't hear. The next time he wouldn't or couldn't hear, the new doctor was told matter-of-factly that last time this had happened, he'd had his Eustachian tube blown out and that had helped. It seemed reasonable, a small cannula, a tube, helped clear out the Eustachian tube again. Next time it was a cold, but mother whispered to a new doctor, "He hates to have his ears blown out, but it always helps." And what competent doctor could avoid asking the boy the same questions that he declined answering so well that he gained the doctor's interference. The family's expectation seemed to leave him little choice. There becomes a lack of hearing from all the probing in his ears, and his ears become a target for every family feud, and he learns to stop listening when the noise level becomes too high. The first ear specialist this boy was sent to was known to the family as a friend because he treated Father's ears. Now there are two generations of blown-out ears and partial deafness.

On the telephone the therapist is easily trapped into perpetuating family circles. Yet here he receives his first impressions, hears for the first time the tone of the family, and begins to make his entrance into their communication system.

Mother calls. "My boy is having trouble at school," she states. "He has guns at home. I am afraid."

"What does your husband say?" I ask.

"He doesn't say," she replies. "He only talks." Her voice is agitated.

A meeting is arranged. Mother is glad that Father is coming. Maybe he will give her some support. Father is glad that he is coming. Maybe Mother will be able to listen.

Mother comes into the office first. She looks tired. Father is upright. Boy is square in body, chunky, walks firmly. Mother tells her story of too many guns. She weeps. Her red-rimmed eyes are set in opal skin, spasmed into helpless folds of sadness at the mouth. Father jets verbal exact directness as he glances out the window. The son mixes glances of concern at Mother and long looks for reassurance from Father. This is not the face of delinquency. This family has a problem of finding one another and communicating effectively what they naturally have to offer and long to share.

A telephone call from another mother. She confides. "His father has always helped Sonnie out of trouble. Can you see him today? Something must be done."

"How old is he?"

"Sixteen. But still in the Juvenile Court," responds Mother. "Do you think it was wrong to protect Sonnie so long?" she asks in a guileless voice.

Father, obsequious in his correctness, has become prominent in the community by being known as honest. Humanity is not his forte: he is honest. Sonnie's early exploration of pennies in Father's pocket was punished by the family court. A cookie filched was a crime against God, duly dealt with by His self-appointed agent. Mother is neither a gun moll nor an accomplice in this God-fearing household, but sometimes she sneaked to Sonnie's side. Father's business clients are churches, which the family attends. Mother, deep in her heart, wonders whether churches aren't entirely clients. Sonnie makes the parents' brutality necessary by his constant testing of their good-evil orientation. It is his way of achieving closeness. The family *machine* is delinquent. The parents and their son together form a training ground as instructive as a penitentiary.

This kind of family does not seek therapy unless the court insists. But the telephone call did not convey this revealing information. The first interview did.

The gun-shy mother sits with her family in my room. This is not a delinquent family. No courts will ever be involved. Here is family misunderstanding: Father's hands are pale, his long arms hang, his mouth moves, giving a clear, blue-eyed precise statement of the family situation. Mother has stopped her red-rimmed weeping; she is gushing emotional tears. Boy has his arm around Mother, hoping to comfort her. His interest in riflery is an effort to direct his own rich emotionalism with a precision like Father's. He shoots high score in his high school rifle club. His heart is torn by Mother's open concern—that a gun is to kill with. This problem of integrating has always pervaded his life. Mother and Father are both warm and intellectual persons. But Mother's tears come sooner than Father's—and he responds to tears by being reasonable. The boy's experience joins his emotion to Ma and his intellect to Pa. He is divided.

The delinquent family and the misunderstanding family are different not only in what they say with words. The boy's arm resting warmly on Mother's shoulder is different from Sonnie's cool fingernail-biting. The gentle-armed boy looks to Father for support. His longing for an answering long look is different from Sonnie's look at his father. In each glance and movement, the delinquent family are sizing one another up; the court, the jury, and the judge trap one another into crimes and punishments written into the family statutes. I seek to produce change rather than explain. But they make me jury.

Faces tense, faces relaxed, arm lying gently on shoulder or in brittle contact—these are observable and familiar to us all. These bits of process from which we make decisions are difficult to describe in formal language.

Family study is a training ground for the observer: the data available are rich.

Sit with a family operating together. Try to determine its traditions. Allow it to happen: it does not take long to experience patterns emerging. You may not know what to name these patterns, but they exist to be named nonetheless.

Everyone knows the reality of a two-person glance: everyone knows the difficulty of putting it into words. The familiar glance within the family defies exposition.

The time-moving process of a family fight, the parents' love match, or their friendship are as difficult to put into words as studying nature in captivity. Telling in words the family's mealtime patterns may be jailing a phenomenon in time as well as confining it in space. Are wrist watch intervals descriptive of the family's go-to-bed story? I am attempting to make the family captive in growth time rather than leaving time dynamics to the regular clock, which bedtime children put to shame. Reader and writer together have a problem of communication: the common knowledge of a hug has a think and feel language that a book about the family must integrate with science.

Boy's worried mother is a heart-feeling person: a Latin by birth, she smells and sweats, loves, cries, and thinks with her body. Her precise husband is Pennsylvania Dutch: he has the coolness and precision of a straight line. No wonder her tears come fast; but his tenderness is wisdom.

"I know he doesn't love me," Latin mother says. "Compared to his people, he is tender and loving, but he never cries, he won't hold me close. Words are for books—he is cold!"

Father's background made him yearn for easy warmth of body that he had not experienced once beyond the Pennsylvania Dutch age for baby-boy hugging. He learned to use words, he married Mother to find her warmth, but he could not learn her language. She used emotion to make simple words more complex in their intellectual meaning; the picture of her changing face made each word a thousand.

Mother looked to straight-line Father for the verbal precision that she felt would allow her to hold her feelings organized enough to manage. Her control faltered when she was not understood.

Boy had to grow ratchetted between these wheels uneasily meshed. Moving in this field between the two wheels, he divided into parts held separate so as to gear with each. There were at least three gear systems implicit in this family's communication: Pennsylvania Dutch, Latin, and a double Interlingua. A not unusual situation, but here they were used as if they held the same grammar customs. Each language structure is a different style of life.

The therapist—a translator at the Tower of Babel—found it his purpose to go beyond the simple quarrel, "Who was right?" He worked to show it is not possible to argue or bargain with coins of different money systems if one *knows* they are the same. If you cannot be aware of different value systems, don't waste your breath on my time. Like all good money changers, the therapist used his expertness to translate the nature of the various coins and their denominations so that each might understand the values of the other. He allowed each to learn to translate for himself the kind of currency they were bargaining with, encouraging them to become experts in this process.

A few months later, Mother began to realize that Father's words *did* mean his love. Her flowing emotionalism was no longer felt by Father as uncertainty or interpreted as anger. It no longer repelled him or prevented his expressing the body warmth possible to his style. And she responded to his words without denying him his body. It could have happened sooner if I knew more about changing.

As the boy of this family recognized the patterns of the conflicts and realized that he had learned them from his need to live between his parents, he began to find his own style. He was able to feel the family's resolution and the gears meshing within himself, and the feeling was so good that he would not play the game of dividing himself into his family members.

You may see "The family is the patient" iterated over and over and over again. And if you are attentive to this concept, you will see the author strain from his own maxim again and again. This is not a book written out of erudition. As you listen to the text, you will hear many strains, some explicit, some implicit, some intentional—and then you will see the back of my head in a way that I myself cannot perceive. The therapist must be aware that he is viewing a family that cannot exist to its own sense as he sees it from outside.

It is time to sell the maxim "Know the other guy!"

Try to imagine what each family member perceives as they sit in their living room. Seen together in my office, a family shows to me, the therapist, aspects of behavior quite unknown to itself, behavior that they cannot report on. The therapist is not just a looking glass, but sometimes he needs only to reflect what the family cannot see. To make contact rather than just use words, he takes the family's own system as test for communication, stretching it where this will strain the implicit into awareness.

Let us turn again to cases.

"What shall we do with Johnny?" a mother asks.

The therapist looks at Johnny, Mother, and Father in one eyeful. "How effective is your family in handling *this* problem?" He had to make this jump, for to respond directly to the question would have meant blindly accepting the family's diagnosis. His emphasis and order of words are intended to suggest that there may be many other issues. The therapist speaks with tone of voice as well as words.

Father responds, "Whom do you expect to reply?"

The therapist: "Whoever is the spokesman for the family."

Father turns scarlet. His eyes narrow as Mother's mouth begins its high-pitched, now apologetic whine. Even as he sits snugged close beside her, she complains of Johnny's distance. The teachers say he is rather feminine. Johnny blows his nose in Mother's scented handkerchief. Father's look of daggers at Johnny, at the scented handkerchief at his nose, at the snuggling-up. This is called by some a castration problem. From day to day this process takes place in the family living room.

"But how effective is the family in handling its problems?" retorts the therapist, knowing full well that he throws off balance the neatly pickled pastimes that the family calls their troubles.

Certain words, phrases, complaints, certain positions and roles, certain stage props—these the family uses to avoid awareness of the operational death it is producing. The therapist focuses back onto the family over and over again: a million devices are being used to seduce him into an individual-controlled, twosome relationship that would have as its purpose *avoiding* the family conflict. Once the family members see themselves—for this therapy—as parts of their family, then the therapist can deal with each member more as an individual.

To return to Johnny's father's groin-cutting looks: the mother is obviously at fault *if* you side with the father, and if you are looking for a fault. Many hard-work interviews later, Father says, "God damn it, why do you use the boy as a substitute for a husband?" Mother says softly, "I wish you had said that a long time ago. I had no one else."

Johnny listens, and by experiencing Father's awareness of Mother's need, his husbanding becomes less necessary. Father's look of daggers was really toward his competitor. Now his son is more than that. Mother-hugging had been the son's way of distracting himself from the awareness of his need to be recognized by Father.

In this Oedipal family, during the long hours when Father,

30

Mother, and Johnny were busy cutting away at each other, I became increasingly aware that each person was trapped in the total family field. As in *Oedipus Rex,* there is no hero and no villain. Everything happens and takes its course while the chorus wails a predicament to the Fates. The family enslavement is strengthened by its own efforts to deal with a significant field dynamic. Wriggling in some nets makes them tighter.

A family symptom: an extending, growing predicament *requires* a self-reinforcing situation in which each effort toward recovery makes the predicament worse. To illustrate: Father, to protect his son from learning from Mother to become a hip-swinging mother's boy, counterbalances her gentling influence by speaking roughly (manly) to his son, who is already afraid. He points up John's lack of manliness by always contrasting his own lean aggressiveness with his son's. To help he told him "Be a man!" It suggests other possibilities. Father avoids contact. He is embarrassed by his son.

Natural progression into ballplaying is hampered by excessive encouragement unrelated to awareness of Johnny's actual achievement.

And Father is so involved with what his son *should be* that he does not know his son. Mother wants her son to be a man, as a man *should be,* not like father. Being a symbol or a cipher is a formality without much fun. Johnny looked for security as he used to know it—the nice skin warmth of a tender mama who was looking for company. Father became more alien, pushing son away, and son turned to his mother, who being more angry at father needed son more, and round and round the circle spiraled.

31

To illustrate again:

The impotent wife's husband, feeling isolated, reaches out for consoling support and moves closer to his wife. Closer, to him, means literally closer. To deal with tension he reduces distance. He clings. When wife is ill or anxious, he surrounds her with soft arms as he wishes to be surrounded when ill himself. But: this wife had been schooled in a family where consideration meant allowing others to lick wounds in private. She tries to give him space so he can pull himself together. This is her way of expressing her considerate love.

The predicament feeds on itself: her husband hurt, she gave him room. Experiencing this as rebuff, he demanded literal closeness, experienced in her system as assault: she hurt more. Feeling his proximity attack her, she needed space; she withdrew. Hurt, he pursued. They came to see the family therapist because they were impotent.

Imagine the potency of two young lovers reaching climax as they warm each other in the round that young lovers know so well. Compare this with the accelerating chase between the hold-hands man and his give-me-room wife: as they run and chase, they sow dragon's teeth and within the form of love's climax multiply—a faster chase. And so breed exhaustion, misunderstanding, reduced communication, powerful hurt, and intrinsic depression. This is an illustration of the two-person self-reinforcing field dynamic.

The three-person field dynamic is more difficult to describe. First, let us hold the model of the previously illustrated two-person dynamic and to it add one child. The clinging father holds the child close, believing that such control is necessary in order that the child may experience love. The mother considerately replies: "Don't smother him;

the child must be given a chance to develop." From the day their child is born, experience teaches him to operate within this divergent field. He becomes an expert at turning up the rheostat of family tension. But that rheostat is numbered 2, 4, 16—and once it passes ignition point 16, the system becomes self-sustaining; he can't turn it down. The chase is faster and no one can get off course. So they begin to drink and stumble, and the son is programmed from an early age in an unusual way.

The sexual experience provides an analogy that is useful in describing growing tension in a family. The growth toward explosion is sometimes extreme.

Some children learn to manage growth toward explosion skillfully and can maintain control by their decision. In a therapy hour, a grown-up tells how she managed to keep the family system from exploding. As she told it to her mother, the grandma now: "If I told you what upset me, you became so much more upset that things got out of hand. So I learned to say nothing. I talked only about neutral things, things that didn't matter." Then she looked at both parents in one eye-view and said, "I could talk to each of you alone: I had my outside friends." She had come to therapy because she wanted her child to have a family feeling. I had asked that the grandparents come as well as spouse and children.

Even as she grew up, she rarely checked or shared with others what counted. Her isolation brought its toll. But this is still not the concept of a family field dynamic. It is a two-and-one, parents to a child, or vice versa. The family is more than that.

Explosion occurs when each person operates in such a way as to enhance the personality swings of the other and there is no control. Shortly there will be no family. Like sulfur, niter, and charcoal rubbed together or jarred from outside stress—explosion. The daughter said, "I didn't ignite the family. I turned to outside friends." The parents and the children were estranged but less explosive. Some families add a buffer to dampen the action within the family. They need neighbors to give sufficient delay time. But sometimes they just explode. There are many techniques for maintaining equilibrium or preventing drift into the explosive range.

Building the concept of the family field of operation are four more kinds of families, familiar to us all but here described within the terms of our new model. Each family exemplifies its own kind of self-revolving system, which controls its course through time.

The Everyone family lives as if the rules of operation were governed by one external organization—the Church, perhaps, or Democracy, or Moral Rectitude. The parents and the children can conduct long dialectics on how *everyone* should be. This dialectical approach provides the padding that prevents realization of both explosive potential and capacity for growth. It is the art of the therapist to unmask the mythology and unleash the explosive toward growth. The Everyone family, padded less, will sometimes declare for Anarchy and test their need for padding. Such families usually have already turned the medical profession into a source of rules for all. Contact with this family's system without becoming an Everyone, an anarchist, or garbage, requires a well-developed sense of humor as well as skill.

The Target family tracks targets against which all the family forces can be directed. One child, one parent, one cause, one illness, are seemingly specific, but whatever is convenient actually is converted into focus. This focus then takes all attention. They lose track of one another except in target practice. They may each destroy the other.

"He is a little nervous." This off-hand comment by the teacher may set him as the target. A diagnosis may call forth its symptom, and the child behaves to fit the role expected.

Target: "Dot was premature," said Mother. "She's been sickly since. Bad chests run in the family. My sister had TB. We always look after her health. She won't play because she doesn't have any muscle coordination. No, she rarely goes out. The children say she doesn't play; it gets so raw outside, and she looks so pale and sickly. She tries to be brave and wants to go out, but we know she just doesn't want us to worry because she isn't well."

The family focuses down on one single event as on a spot. They do not see the spiral, the reinforcement, over time.

If this focusing is matched by a response that reinforces expectation, finally (for the Target people) there can be built within the vicious cycle a logic that seems unassailable: Dot becomes ill as expected.

The Narrows use a third mode of holding their vital force in check. Within this family there is a simple system that explains all behaviors: activity is examined through a polarizing lens.

Sexual "morality" is the heart of the Narrows family. When the male son first draws, the inevitable pencil slip between the legs is *hastily* rubbed out. His hands are tied to prevent him from exploring the filthy holy of holies. The female daughter is warned endlessly, from five years on, "You must not become pregnant." The parents keep preparing for the final leap. It is taught by its "prevention." At the breakfast table, the parents smile in horror as they read in the morning paper about the church-going Boy Scout, always nice to his mother, who is alleged to have committed some sexual crime. The narrow band of polarization combines prevention with expectation, and each begets its opposite.

In this kind of family, parents and children divide into teams of opposites. For them the world has two sides, and all communication between them is in terms of "Crime versus Sweetness" or "She hasn't lost it yet." It is a form of training by omission of neutral territory.

The Ought-to family live by "Should" and "Might." Their world is designed by the logic of obligation and rewards. There is no chance of happenstance. These are the anti-existentialists who watch a crime for what it represents. Self-righteous discussion is the key. They explain: "A crime of passion ought to be punished *or* ought to be understood."

Their life is but a series of highly abstract judgments. Everything is carried into abstract discussion to teach everyone forever. The Ought-to family may not relate to its children before they become verbal—and, lacking contact, these children may never become truly verbal. Instead, they use inexperienced labels to play, with family pride, the game. They confound the others with abstractions unconnected with experience. Sensory deprivation may occur where contacting warmth does not counteract ephemeral abstractions. To keep in contact, labeling and living must enrich each other.

In these samples you will catch the beginning flavor of many kinds of families. Each family has its own personality and its own culture, and this culture builds with each unfolding moment. Behavioral evolution in a family is a biological process. As we proceed, this process will unfold.

we meet on more channels

WALKING TO MY WAITING ROOM I see a new family sitting quietly, all reading. They are plump in their chairs, relaxed. Well-dressed and manicured, gray-striped Father, bright-red-jacketed son, brass-buttoned. The sister sits erect, a teen-ager, voluptuously combining the best features of her mother and her father, smiling serenely like a madonna or a store-window dummy. There is a calm shaking of hands, warm, but shyly held by Brass Buttons. Calmly across the stage they walk, into my office, as if well tutored by a better charm school. My abstract painting over the fireplace gets a quick scrutiny from perceptive eyes. "I like it," says the father. Brass-buttoned boy fidgets. Father glowers and launches into a droning monologue recounting how much he has done for the family, and his son can't even sit still when he's told. Mother fidgets. Sister fidgets. I fidget. Brass Buttons gets a twinkle in his eye. Has he become aware that anything he does to discomfort Father will begin a break for Mother—a silent sigh of relief? He fidgets louder. Father paces lecture halls, then leaps upward to ecclesiastic pulpits. Father's isolation makes you more confused . . . empty resonance bouncing from pews. Father is depressed, his words are out of contact. They are all silent, hurt and unspeaking—wanting to protect him. His voice trails off. Silence.

"Father is right," replies Mother, looking directly at her son, hoping that he will be aware she is only saying what is necessary. After all, she is a wife as well as his mother. She soon falls silent, leaving silence to be filled by silence filling pulpit words more lofty—out of contact. They are all afraid of gargoyles. Gargoyles on the ceiling loom as funny friends to frighten off evil conflicts.

Brass Buttons has no friends to play with: he is untrained to fight. He is eight. He is in public school, and "He has fallen silent," the teacher says, "and talks to himself." Model sister slowly says, "My brother bothers me. I wish he had a life of his own." Therapist: "My, you are a polite family. Everyone seems so understanding." Mother's Irish is exposed by flushing cheeks. She slowly supports her husband's interruption: his diagnosis of his son. I gently point out that as a family they are not much for entertaining. Mother responds, "Father has so few friends. Perhaps because I did not go to college."

The office of a family therapist has more chairs than most, and usefully the chairs have different status value. My own chair I consider neutral—though truly I don't believe that is true. My desk chair leans back, and is usually occupied by father or son. It is higher. The traditional couch holds two or three. It is opposite me. And on the other side of the fireplace is the comfortable chair. Like the three bears, each person of the family soon finds his own chair. Children find supports for their bottoms . . . perhaps on a lap. A child on the floor has his own special plane, which the adults rarely share. On my work desk are some simple blocks and crayons: the family is invited to bring its favorite toys.

Sitting around a table in the middle of the room might be useful to some, but for me it would be like wearing my glasses and ears half blackened. Tables hide activity. Family therapy depends upon awareness of interpersonal action in the open. I have a glass coffee table, which sets a center for the family circle. It is free-form and does not impose a rectilinear structure on the group as a wooden table would.

The way a family structures their geometry of space is an important information. Brass Buttons sits roundly cuddled up to Father as he lectures. This act of space belies the vaulted tones. If Mother had sat on the couch, would son have cuddled up to her? I think not. Brass Buttons' relationship to his father reminds one later of Mother and Father's earlier hand-arm holding as they walked into the room. In spite of words, these people are genuinely close. Sitting in my chair I feel the radiant warmth flowing between them. There are no cold, pale, or spasmed skins among them. Father is not so caught up with, as trapped by, his own preaching.

For contrast, let the next new family arrive: father, mother, eight-year-old son, and seven-year-old daughter. Father thin, lanky, pinched cheeks—a cold hand with a covered-voice hello. His fingers are long and tense—stringy muscles. His face is stretched over with leathery skin. There

41

is a slight twitching upturn of the mouth toward sniffing nostrils. The chair is hardly dented by his alertness. Mother's mouth droops, but teeth are held tight. She is determined but used to defeat. Her lids are red. Her dress is carefully chosen to save money. The two children, Hansel and Gretel, hang on to each other by fighting. Speaking indefinitely, Father leads the way with accusation. The boy's eyes dart, but his limbs hang loose in pathetic bewilderment. The girl sits quietly smiling at her defeated mother. The family is in pieces.

"I was right." "No!" "I am right." "No!" Turning to me, "He is wrong." "No. She is wrong." This is the substance of the conversation. Illustrations accurately drawn from the lawyer's-evidence type of mind reduced to "Who is right?" The therapist's chair rises as he sits behind the bench making judgments. As he maneuvers to escape the bench, he passes through a feeling of absence of position from which to say *anything*.

"She is castrating me," he accuses. "I can do nothing to please him," she replies.

The children cling to each other. Being well trained in the social virtues, the therapist feels cruel allowing children to witness parents' deadly struggle. Warmth drains from my skin, my stomach quivers. Their voices hiss a high-pitched rip of bleeding, tatters, whining.

This is one level of the problem I deal with. To say "Stop" will delay my understanding of their way of life. I must make my move from their strength, which they are hiding.

Protecting children from one hour of listening to the fighting that has gone on all their lives is only protecting the therapist whose own vitality is being offended. The therapist must experience enough of the family fear, sadistic rage, and isolation to make contact with the family's reality. He must be skilled enough at his own protection to remain optimally in contact with their reality and with his own. This is a therapist's function. One teaches by example. To control them (if he could) would be to prevent his own experience of what goes on every day in this family's home. This display is necessary at the start, but by itself is not therapeutic. They have not come for his control, for one day's help, but for change. To allow the old fight to continue without useful intervention is to use up energy for nothing. But the intervention must be designed to break the family system from its old rut into self-sustaining change. This is the challenge. It is more than encouraging "expression."

Whatever the children say, the mother and father fight about it. The words are rigged into old actions, which circulate to keep the fires of conflict burning. Each family member needs the other's support. What parents may name in their children as symptoms are commonly the children's way of coping—as they deem necessary for family survival. If one sets the premise to be "Find the sick individual," one may never become aware of such health as exists in the total family climate. The spirit of Brass Buttons' family contrasts with the spirit of Hansel and Gretel. Stone gargoyles are not witches. Hansel and Gretel are in danger of being chewed up into strings—Mother and Father are already corpsed. Brass Buttons feels the warmth of Father's skin, knows the softness of his reassuring presence, and needs not glint his eye to ward off danger. His muscles move with ease, their bodies with fluidity, and the madonna teen-age sister, though acting like a dummy, is not made of plastic. She has been modeling to earn extra spending money. Brass Buttons' family is rich; they also have money. Hansel and Gretel come from a poor, hungry woodcutter's family, where every member focuses on searching out the pebbled droppings whose magic is to bring them to wealth and out of danger. The fantasy wealth of sugarplums and gingerbread by contrast bleakens the cold, foodless cottage; pebbles lead the way— the woodcutter's family cannot break out of their impoverished system. The therapist's task is simple with Brass Buttons, but it is frightening with the family that has been frozen by several generations of deprivation.

These two families illustrate two forms of self-reinforcing systems, two different forms. Hansel and Gretel are to most the heroes of their story. But the stepmother and father had a practical problem. There was not enough bread in the house. Did the children go out and earn some? Give their parents warmth? No. They took off to the witch's and gave no reward to their parents, reinforcing and making real a family-shared myth.

Let us turn aside for a moment to illustrate self-reinforcement. A baby crying in the park can make a mother miserable. She gently rockaby-babies the carriage, warming his food. But raucous cries, the wails of what sounds like an uncared-for child, bring public censure. And guilt turns a look of placid disapproval from mothers with placid children to a look of disdain, which makes more tense the shoving of the carriage back and forth. Baby, now tired of crying, responds to the bumping with louder, thinner wails, psychologically undermining the natural animal-mother feelings of all the mothers in the park in spite of their private ownership of children declared by birth certificates and other social rules. Sometimes holding and cooing breaks the cycle. But the tenser children in a tense situation have the knack of making it worse, turning the wheel a little faster. A mother jangled by the racking wails comes clacking home, cooks a miserable meal, finds no comfort in her husband's angry silence. This child, well schooled, soon learns that the slave controls the jailer, that Cinderella made the sisters wicked, and that a dried-up-looking child makes any parent feel evil.

Hansel and his mate Gretel—the two children clinging to each other on my couch—make each parent sure that one of them must be an evil stepmother or a witch. The round of stated and unstated accusations continues, and the therapist may find no way to break through.

One month after therapy begins, our Brass Buttons boy has come alive within his family. He has managed to show his father that he considers the old man a good guy. And Father has begun to listen. Father beams with satisfaction. He weeps with pleasure. The son dares to generate his own private kind of life: no longer silent, he is drawn by others' listening to begin more activities about which to tell the listeners. The family spiral reverses as the increased freedom of the family catalyzes further freedom to undress their strength. Brass Buttons wears dungarees. He walks like a boy at home and tells at home that his friends have always liked him. Friends did exist: he had not known. The parents glow with pride. Each discovery of being healthier accelerates the growth of further change.

In the Hansel and Gretel family, the growth toward further illness remained the prominent direction of self-reinforcement.

The family therapist must be aware from the first hour of his own tendencies or he will find himself listening exclusively to one particular family member and filtering the others through that one's grid. The arrangement of office props can assist or detract from a family-unit focus. One learns in the first hour of therapy to maximize unspoken aids to family focus. A family member sitting directly opposite, face to face, will make it almost impossible to listen to another family member sitting at right angles. A turn of the therapist's head, which loses a piece of family from his visual field, loses him contact with the family organism, particularly if he or the family requires eye-to-eye contact for intimate communication. I find it best to sit far enough back from the family group to be able to include it all in one glance. Using my peripheral vision, I can observe the movements of the family members as they coordinate rhythmically in their family dance. Ears to father and eyes into his, I may lose the puzzled up-and-down listening to mother's high-heeled foot, which father decodes as he takes his next breath.

He continues. She plants the balls of her feet firmly on the ground. Simultaneously I meld mother's story of the truth to father's glance at little boy's paying-back-sister slap. Instead of questioning mother's irritatingly correct sense of truth, I merely state, "While Mrs. Truth was talking, Mr. Truth was not listening. He speaks by his style of controlling the children. Who listens in this family?"

Even in the first hour's interview, the therapist checks out the capacity for shift. Verbal shift is not prognostic. It is the shift in spirit and tone that must be read, the spirit of that part of the family so basic that it looks like them—they all walk like that. The record of anxiety, anger, or love—it is not words. A sudden laugh of free chest pleasure breaks into the script of usual rattle.

In the first interview, one begins to predict. It is the moment-to-moment shifts in the progression of unintentional messages sent by the family organism that serve to focus the remainder into predictive information. Prediction of capacity for basic change is not revealed by that which is intended. The instrument of family progress is breadth of a relationship rather than the first hour's defined narrowness of conflict—the major complaint. Sometimes the stated conflict does leech out contact with the daily change progression necessary to a growing family life. But this is a special case. The productive constancy of a living thing is change and growth.

Even in the first hour one attends to time itself as it flows through the family constellation, changing, building, breaking down. One listens to a moment-to-moment phrasings, the corrections within the family system that define its course. Do phrases appropriate to one moment successfully happening continue to be "successful" too long and lose contact with time? A timeless happy childhood is not the finest preparation for the real world: mother enters, carrying thirty-year-old child in maternal bliss. A family must change from year to year and hour to hour. And moment to moment.

It is breakthrough contact with authentic feelings and old schoolings now languaged into life's grammar that augurs change.

While the therapist observes, he gains information of what the family remembers.

At the first interview, I inquire of the family's home address, addressing my question to the whole family so as to notice which member of the family replies. Is the question of the location of the family home answered by mother, while Johnny sits silent? Does father reply before mother can get the words out? Is the address given precisely? and how long has the family lived in this home? Were the children born there? When did the family begin to exist as such? Was the courtship long? And how old were you both? Where from—the country or the city—and what did you work at then, and how is the family organized in terms of income production now? There are different styles, depending on the style of the family. The old family physician visiting the home was trained in the art of building a history of the family by questioning the individual while watching the total family respond. This art now becomes overt technique.

The family's chief complaint is seen in relief within the total communication that is observed.

My head apparently buried in the pad of paper to write down notes may be a device to help avoid taking over direction of the one who will answer as the momentary mouthpiece of the family.

I construct in my notes a genealogical chart, which in the manner of genealogical charts runs for several generations. After placing on the chart the names, ages, and occupations of the present family members, I inquire, sometimes dryly, of the grandparents, uncles and aunts, and other members of the family tree. This will be the basis for the fleshing out of the family. Such a chart would not be complete without the writing in of dates of deaths as well as births, of family fortunes, of who got on with whom, and which ones got married. And most important of all, small notations are made as to how the verbal story is emotionally structured.

What is your occupation? Where do you work? What part of the country did your family come from? Was your family immigrant or native? Religion? All such data as can be briefly sampled are elicited. This family history is but a beginning: it will mushroom out as more detail becomes available, and then charts would take a different form, showing feedback loops, control systems, explosion points etc., etc. This is a beginning of the complex of information that the therapist must deal with in his head. The therapist needs his thoughts to net out those facts he will build into relevance, correcting as the incongruent data create new predominant patterns.

Its words apart, the family as it operates together within the room unintentionally presents to the therapist a brand of information incongruent with the family's verbal system.

Family education? A mother whinnies with laughter as Father spontaneously describes the embarrassment of his college when he got straight A's—after being threatened with expulsion! She enjoys his bawdy life, told in front of the children, who respond as though used to bawdiness and challenge. This family is already operating more effectively than its neighbors. The professor is not satisfied. He is as dissatisfied as he was with the college that he led into his trap. "Make fools out of fools," he declares, "and let's get things done." The family is together in joining both tasks; it is not hard to assist the production toward greater productivity, but it is harder to write about such a pleasant operation. It began in the first interview with the question of family education. I did not stop the flow.

Father talks unreservedly about his learning relationship with his own father, also a professor, too damn busy with the business of the college to be a family man. Mother speaks of education as warmly as of her family life. I see no reason to question her account: some lives are happy and still reach out for more. The listening children, twelve and eight, learn in detail of their heritage and with this new information see their parents less as strangers. "We know each other better now," the family tells me as they leave, and I have helped them find words with which to talk about what they shared before more vaguely. The courage to expect what one has not as yet achieved brings some families to family therapy.

But there are other families where the human story is more somber. The next family came from a small town. Their boy is in a special class. The teachers object because he is not doing well. Father: "He is just like me—I never did well either." Mother: "I should have warned him about school: I told him he would have to learn to lace his shoes before he went. He understood. He always understands me. We changed teachers. The first one couldn't handle him. He enjoys parachutes."

Father is a pleasant-looking man. He looks mildly, speaks mildly, his body is like pudding. Mother sits plumpishly pleased with a son who is her son—not Teacher's. "They say he is very sick." Father: "He is just like me." "Parachutes?" I ask quietly. "Oh, yes," Mother replies. "He has one to play with."

Nobody is displeased except school. The boy stands by the window, muttering, to amuse himself, I guess. He slips in and out of focus. His preoccupation in the last few months has been parachutes. "He has no friends, he isn't learning in school," his teachers say. But there is no urgency in the family. The family is satisfied, but I wonder where they are going. Is a boy sick who is an adequate representation of his own family's style?

The sense of urgency is omitted from this family's escutcheon: the control necessary for contact with organization outside the family's unusual structure is hampered. This is not a lack of discipline: spanking Johnny when he is bad is *done,* but there is no sense of urgency, no spankings for something defined by outside. The family is not urgently interested in what is significant to the school. To them, creativeness and the boy's own thoughts are all that is important. Will he be a character who discovers what traditional education would destroy? There is no passion. When a family is satisfied, a family interview does not easily build crisis. What is there to resolve? Bringing in the teacher as a part of the group might bring in conflict. But this family seems to share its own special values. No crisis, no work. The local net of communication within the family is in good order; the family organism itself is called into question by those on the outside.

The first listening is to history reenacted as it is told. Does Mother's voice get smaller as she remembers her weenie infant, now sitting teen-aged before her? Does Father's information peter out, and then does he smile with the solicitude of a mother as he remembers getting up at night while Mother worked all day? Is the child embarrassed by hearing for the first time the story of his parents' engagement, that they met at the Officers' Club or on a blind date? You may ask—most people do—"Should little ears be told?" I reply: "Should children have heard about their parents' childhood only from overhearing?" How often do our children disappear from our awareness when we are seriously confiding? Out of sight is not out of earshot, and they listen even while they play inattentive. Then they have no opportunity to correct by sharing that which they are not supposed to know. Mother speaks with embarrassment of how Aunt Sue got sick and died in their home. The children were upstairs.

"They knew nothing about what was going on." Mother reassures me. The children, now older, snicker and correct Mother's statement that it was in the afternoon. In the same home, no one speaks of Grandmother's blindness; it has never been mentioned. Mother proudly states: "She knows her room so well that the children surely don't know that she cannot see."

The boy winks at me.

So often the real secret is that everyone knows that there isn't a secret. The boy winked at me. And they all wink at one another, pretending that a most obvious knowledge doesn't exist—and this prevents contact.

In the first hour the listening therapist tries to assess the family's traditions as to what is known. If unintentionally the therapist grossly oversteps their code, they will not return. In many families, easily inferred information may be maintained outside open discussion and even awareness. It is the therapist's work to understand the family censorship code and to make them aware of it; it is not his function to change it, although such discovery usually brings changes.

The therapist can often guess what everyone knows but leaves unsaid—each believing that theirs is private information. The utility of checking out with real questions—daring to ask what has never been asked before—can be early demonstrated. My question, then, will be so directed as to test what happens when I poke ever so slightly in this silent area. Does the family burst into talk about something else? Respond by attack? Or are they eager to discover what they had accommodated long ago—to jump over this hampering wall and explore with one another a field left fallow now without reason?

Some areas of silence will remain silent: the privacy of individuals is not always the business of the family group. But while the verbal report may be denied, communication of significant events is usually revealed in the action sequence. Yes, communication is action. Last night's frustration in bed may not be spoken of to the children except as "No, it was not your homework. I was talking with Mother." Sometimes the whole discussion is wordless, perhaps a smile that profoundly corrects misunderstanding.

Action communication is usually taught by apprenticeship. It is the art of the family. But though it is called "intuitive," it is messages sent and received as learned over time . . . the nuance of muscle strands held tense . . . a neck flushed . . . eyes focused on each other or seeing through the window, or through the past into nothing, or into fear of fire-burning hate and destruction. The therapist can begin in the first hour to decipher the system.

Those who family together know the contact seemingly long forgotten but well learned on the lap, child's cheek to mother's in a resting position. The wordless child held close to the unworded diameter of the mother's pupil, sees lightening and darkening of her iris—brown to hazel—and eye whites turning pink as vessels dilate ready to cry at Father's voice. Shininess wells long before tears ever drop. Face to close face, children learn parents' sensitivity. And how wide are the eyes open, protruding or relaxed? Muscles at the corner of the eye slitting it down into suspicion. Lap muscles ready to jump and give protection. How often do you think of what a child is seeing as you hold him in your arms? Intuition, the wordless contact of eye-and-lap patterning, is organized into the family's nonlingual language.

Eyes jerk from side to side in fearful glances, and these eyes see another world than does an eye that integrates into musical wholeness. It is from this base over several generations that the family pattern builds. It takes more than one generation to break a cultural pattern. For example, is someone listening if his hands are busy? In some traditions, yes, in other, no.

The therapist's first fifty-minute photograph is one frame of the family's lifelong motion picture. If the observer sees the motion in this frame, he sees more than any static, formal fifty minutes' worth of words can ever define, but for this art—a human-species form—there is so little language.

Joining the hands of every family member into one perception is a part of family contact. It is the progressing dance of all the hands, the still growing pace rather than one particular movement or its avowed purpose, that one follows.

Does the family move together? As one? Randomly disconnected? Swinging together? Wet blanket?

A father and son avoid embrace. Their warm hands gently touching belie all words of distance. Notice—he is tense, while she clutches the arm of the chair, flesh flattened by pressure.

Am I just an advocate of careful observation?
No.

People are the movements. The family flows through time as action. Watch! The hands that clutch the chair once held the child.

This family's skin is warm, thick, and dry. And nails are red with polish. The prognosis is different from that of the family which is warm and pink, less aged by death.

Sniff! No smell, but watch the underarm stain grow larger. Why be polite? "Is this a signal when you are tense?" The others laugh. They know how to use that sign, but who would think to mention it?

The wife didn't know what the therapist saw in the first interview that gave him a lead. "How are you able to know so much? We have told you so little." I watched her husband's eyelids' sudden rapid flutter underline the points of conflict. I asked, "Was she aware of this eye language?" She spoke with surprise: "I had never listened." Later I learned she couldn't receive this message, she hadn't learned how. For many years she had seen no detail of his face. Then she bought contact lenses.

As I watch a family in process for just one hour, I become aware that psychological theories that teach as though thoughts were something and flesh nothing are making a separation less than useful, in fact, impossible. This awareness is a practical matter in the designing of research to learn about family life. Questionnaires about what families think give a brand of information unlike questionnaires asking what they are doing, which is again very different from how they show what they are doing by the way, unwittingly, they use the spaces of the questionnaire—or divide the seats in my office.

When I see the family operate together, I see thrown into highlight their professional family values, their mythology contrasted with their operational process over time. The family's mythology is usually apparent in the first hour. Asking the simple question, "What kind of family are you?" can set the tone at once.

Unlike the more classical "Tell me about yourself," this other question often brings a discussion of function that is entirely oversimplified but that sets a question. And this question may remain at the heart of the work.

What kind of family? What is your style? How do you live? This is not easy to decipher, for the code lies in the paper and ink of the system rather than in the neatest of scrawlings. Each family has its own Holy Ghost. Though often glibly known and named, even formalized in a common family emblem, the Holy Ghost, an ethereal substance that pervades the family structure, is so intrinsic and vital as to be unknown. The analogy to the Holy Ghost is not unfounded, for in the religious idiom the Holy Ghost is similarly omnipresent, a named presence that can be experienced by those who belong, although its operations are "beyond knowing."

families
in
process

HEAVINESS HUNG around the room. There was nothing special in what the family said, but the heaviness persisted. It had seemed to arrive with them. "I sense a pall of heaviness in the room," the therapist said. He knew the family well, it was not the first interview. "Is this just my own personal reaction? Or is there something serious going on that we're not talking about? The weight feels to me like a thousand pounds of worry, and I cannot account for more than five hundred in myself."

The family looks surprised. They are not used to talking about their feelings. They have had no time for it.

They ponderously respond with talk of their necessity. Necessities are necessary to earn. Feelings are not necessary. Father's business simply must have Mother's support. The daughter, aged sixteen, is very slow. She takes an hour to plan anything, checking so it won't go wrong. The son, younger, has friends outside the house. He teases his sister and gibes at her slowness. She checks again to be sure she won't be wrong. For two hours a week, this family sits in my office, taking the time to consider their family way of life.

"They are crazy serious," says the boy. "I get out. Other kids' families have fun."

Seriousness becomes a topic of consideration. This conversation would not have taken place at home in this family. The therapist has a chance to make possible and to hear family discussions that are different from those at home. The son who is always out is here: he can't get out of this. But here there is perspective, so he is not flooded out. As the hour develops, the slow daughter manifests her slowness as response, and I become aware that complex pacing is used to form a language of slow-fast rates, encoded and decoded with exactness by all the family. My comment about feeling has slowed the pace. I focus on pace as the feeling exchange. Before, the family had not been aware of its use of pace as language. Its rules of grammar now begin to grow to awareness.

The family in its relationship to me, an outsider hired to help them, focuses on the problems they experience as they operate together in my office. I try to help them discover their implicit operations, some of which they find inappropriate to their ongoing life. The family presence together as a unit is itself an important part of family therapy. The family struggles with common problems and, with me, works together to discover its usual system—its own structure.

There is resistance to making explicit the implicit. A struggle, underground before but now conceptualized, turned around, and looked at again and again at different times and

58

from different times and from different points of vantage, erupts into being more directly experienced. Rules no longer taken for granted can be tested and understood. The therapist, to facilitate, may tell a crucial joke when the family is most serious. The timed lightness of his humor, by contrast with the family tone, is itself a comment.

The beginning of the hour is a time for therapist listening. I notice that each family member acts then as if the others were not present, referring to "he" or "she" as if the other were at home, though they sit side by side. The therapist may simply wait and watch till suddenly one family member meets another in his room. Then he underlines the meeting with a comment that facilitates the meeting process. The art is the acknowledgment of emerging points of change.

The Serious family has gradually worked its way into this predicament. Father and Mother and Brother can be gay outside the family circle. Sister has not reached beyond the family circle; as her brother says, "She's a square." Her lack of gaiety contrasts with the others' efforts to escape seriousness, and she has contraverted fun into mere frivolity, which she considers silly. And the other family members are afraid of being considered silly fools. Who can be spontaneous in a wet blanket's presence? And she follows their example.

The family has drifted over time toward seriousness. Gratification of basic human needs had become an item of superfluous furniture. Joy has been so concretized into blocks of feelingless words that having fun is now on purpose because for health's sake everyone should have fun. . . . It doesn't work that way.

The Serious family is not so serious as to be unaware of its predicament. They just don't know how to get out of the circular drift.

"Did you *ever* have fun?" I ask at a time when the family is getting more and more concerned about starting to have fun.

"I used to tell my daughter stories," Mother answers.

"We always talk before she goes to bed," Daughter adds. "Then Mother says it's bedtime at nine-thirty. I've never said this before, Doctor, but I think she's really just bored with me."

Mother is sitting beside her but holds herself still, not daring to respond. But in the next interview Mrs. Serious answers: "I no longer care about my daughter's bedtime. It had become routine. After all, she's sixteen now."

The daughter proudly adds: "I went off to the store and spent *all* the money."

"What thievery is this?" the therapist jokes. She has complained that Mother controls the money, and I am curious to develop what that means.

Mother explains, "I gave her money to buy her own clothes. She did a good job."

A change is beginning. Quickly Father slows down the pace with an old repetition, "She always gets up so slowly. I always awaken the children in the morning to see that they awake on time for school."

"Do the children not like school?" I ask.

"They like school," Father replies.

"Would you get yourselves up?" I ask the children.

"He wakes us," they reply.

"Another circle," I respond amused.

A habit, a tradition of who wakes whom, can remain with a family and continue long after its usefulness is past. Some families collect old furniture, books, and papers. Their attics are full of things never thrown out—fire hazards. Old rules can stultify a family's growth, and yet the family becomes so used to them that only the outsider can bring this to their attention.

One father, when talking about the function of the therapist, told of his own experience as a coordinator for a series of chain stores. He said, "When I arrived at the next chain store after a long winter drive, I would notice the sign above the door, 'New fall styles are here.' A glance toward the sign would make the store manager aware of its long-forgotten presence. Just talking about things as we do here makes them change." Accommodation to what was once useful leaves one unable to cast off old patterns.

Most families are not so easy to deal with as the Serious family. Nor can the symptoms be a reliable guide to the potential for change. The heaviness, the false seriousness experienced when they first came into the room makes the therapist overserious about what will happen. His testing in the first two hours, rather than the family's self-appraisal, is likely to give an accurate guide to the gravity of the predicament in which the family is caught. He asks himself how completely is the family caught in its own web of energy-consuming mythologies? Each image of what should be may deny the reality of what is happening.

The hummingbird stands still midair by fluttering—a family may seem still because it maintains fatiguing, high-velocity stabilizing dynamics. The plummet to health or sickness cannot be predicted by the family's own description of itself. The family pays for the therapist's expert capacity to perceive the unintentional flutter whose tiniest breath guides his next searching movement.

Each family has its own particular game, its rules and regulations. It has its rules of status, its rules of power, its techniques of movements. There are implicit regulations that govern how many are allowed to participate at once, and how to win. As with most games there is an established objective. The game in each family is a function of their social group. The character of a family's system must be backgrounded by an awareness of the customs of its social group. Each family uses its background in its particular way.

The Quiet family. They manage to get along with everyone else in the community. They are considered respectable but dull. In the office, Father unfolds dullness into some vitality. An avowed objective is defined—not to hurt the others. This is accomplished by withdrawing hurtful information from the family exchange system, anything that has not been already said may be hurtful, and all potential zip is jailed in silence. Enforcements for the control of zip guns have stopped the citizenry from talking loudly in the street. These regulations were never posted. The therapist's job at first is to pick up the slightest signs of unquiet. Long pauses are common. But a smile thickened by teeth and jaws ready to bite is commented on by the therapist as it becomes more and more inappropriate to the needling that is really taking place. Mother admits, "I hate that smile, it's so damn insincere"—the beginning of a breakthrough.

The Quiet family tentatively begins with tiny sleet-needle swipes, then it tries pea-shooting, then hastily retreats to unctuousness. The therapist responds to this movement only by return of like—smiling ever so unctuously, as if he were a mirror, but speaking with his face, not saying a word. The equally smiling husband takes no notice: the wife side glances to see my imitative smile: her equilibrium is noticeably upset. She is aware of her husband's unawareness and what was her own. Now the task is hers to break the mask, and the therapist repeatedly tunes into the family's own system discordantly to ask: "How does the family deal with cover-up emotions?"

This is a slow, many-interview process, rewarded as one's knowledge of the family allows increasingly refined interventions—moving toward making intentional implicit operations and giving new choices.

The family therapist has as his function making conscious the unconscious family dynamics. Using the field concept, this means making aspects of the family operations that were previously unknown to the family, out-of-awareness, available to scrutiny and decision.

The individual therapist will be uncomfortable with the concept of a family unconscious. Such a concept is inevitable, however, if we consider that each family member is in dynamic exchange with the others in terms of his own personality, which in large measure is unconscious. Those who do not like the term "family unconscious" or "group unconscious" or the Jungian concepts, which are similar, can use other words. The therapist's primary job remains that of bringing into awareness aspects of the family operations that are unintentional. In the process, he becomes, inevitably, a student of the complexities of human communication.

Usually, each family member has a particular segment of

the total family interaction that he is especially aware of. He likewise has a particular area, a particular level, about which he is particularly dense. The presence of all the family members in one room together, and the gradual establishment of communication contact between them, when the focus is on the family functioning, bring the maximal amount of awareness to bear upon the maximal amount of obliviousness.

Capacity to tune delicately into one another's vulnerability develops over time in any family.

The capacity to use the others' vulnerability in an emotional manner is illustrated in the solar-plexus punch. It is a family operation common to all, a sneaky operation that illustrates the balance-maintaining mechanics of a central conflict. Pointing out such process can bring new information about why it was used and how. Mr. Brown tells of solar plexus sinking into doubled-up helplessness. "I felt wonderful when I first got home," he reports, "but three words from my wife and I crumpled. She said nothing bad, she was cheerful. She only said, 'You had *another* hard day at the office, honey?' I remembered all the miseries that this day I had defeated. I recovered till I sat down at the table. Then she said graciously, 'Would you like some sugar in your tea?' After years and years she doesn't know. 'Did I do something wrong, honey? You seem upset.' "

The solar-plexus punch is a powerful blow. There is the sense of helplessness and sudden loss of contact with someone who is supposed to be important. The blow is silent. There seems no one to get back at. One feels yet, the pain below. Is something wrong? What happened? Nothing of

64

meaning. I feel depressed. Am I breaking up? Should I feel grateful? What was said was trivial.

It takes two to tangle, and the solar-plexus punch requires a puncher and a punchee. A family is a family for a long time. Some families grow in awareness of one another's strengths, but expertise in vulnerabilities grows apace. The solar-plexus punch depends upon a concatenation of innuendoes delicately placed to disembowel the sturdiest other. Like cyanide in bonbons, nothing shows.

The one punched can receive the blow only when he is set up paunchy ready. To be hurt, one must be unsure of one's own ground, vulnerable not necessarily about that which is brought into focus by the other's comment, but rather vulnerable in the fear of a sudden shift in a frame of reference. There is sudden dissolution of a way of coping that had been solid, and exposure of usually covered rawness within.

The day has gone well, and the evening meal is in process. The pace is happy, the music light, the telephone rings. Mother-in-law from a thousand miles away simply says, "It's *so* nice to hear your voice *again*." Her tone and emphasis set off memory of a thousand obligations purposively forgotten in the enjoyment of the evening. And one's soul fills with impotent rage. A self-reinforcing sense of guilt that each of us has experienced makes one forget why one has made the reasonable decision not to write or call. Doubled in pain, a wife again becomes a daughter, and she may then slug her husband with a solar-plexus punch.

The solar-plexus punch is worth pursuing here, not because the dynamics are understood in detail, but because it is a common phenomenon. There are other families, though, a less common kind, where the thump in the belly of the solar-plexus punch is *the* way of life, not an expression of a particular self-correcting mood.

Sitting with the Mace family over long periods of time, one gradually becomes aware that all the family members are well armed. The daughter of this family has been called schizophrenic. "She is out of contact," the family was told, "and should be hospitalized." Yet she had the greatest awareness of those family operations which were unknown to other family members: and to those who had seen her without the whole family present, what seemed her fanciful description was the closest one could touch the actual situation.

Her father in the interview shakes his finger at his daughter—it is his symbol of his out-of-contact authority. He screams with his finger as if it were a mace, a spiked club. A father who shakes his pen at Mother and the children may get his tie cut off. The tie, like the fasces, like the mace, like the pointed pen or finger, is used to deny and extinguish awareness of his real longing for contact with his family. Father could insist only by his authority that he had a right to exist for his family—but the family he wanted to exist for lived only in his mind.

The Mace mother was a milk squirter, squirting milk like a fire hose controlling a mob. This was her way of trying to give what she wanted for herself and didn't have.

The college son had deserted.

The high school girl-child was alternately maced and squirted. But within the pressure of the clobber and the balm, she made her nest, dancing a weird dance that used as its music and rhythm the unconscious family interplay.

To conceptualize this three-person melee strains the capacity of our language. The girl spoke in metaphors as if reading in a magic mirror the ancient days of Rome.

How is a mirror a weapon? The mirror held at a particular angle makes it possible to reflect to another a particular facet of his (or her) personality about which he feels completely vulnerable. This is one kind of solar-plexus punch. The mirror accurately reflects Father's swipe with the mace. His sadism in the name of honor and control is mirrored by making more control necessary until his position is clearly sadistic. Without torment, Father would be able to control this side of his character.

In the family dance, each family member metaphorically kicks the other in his vulnerable response to being kicked. But they live their lives in a metaphoric language, and each kick hurts. The girl tries to escape by ridiculing the logic that would make the world a world of reason. And the kicking persists even as it is denied by being experienced as a sequential response to each other's defensive kicking.

Aristotelianism, the separation of flux into parts, the rose from its stem, can allow a strange reality to be formed in the family and yet be internally logical until it bursts into florid psychosis. And the restrictiveness of a paranoid painting her hair-black lines, each accurately placed to be exact, is menacingly unreal.

And Mother squirts her hose in a long stream of milk, which blinds the children's eyes to the world outside. The nineteen-year-old is squirted into the mirror oblivion that she long ago assumed. Her outside friends were never friends but extensions of a family expectation couched in reflecting friendliness.

Contrast the above therapist's description in its pace and intensity, with the helpful father's statement. "As a father I expect to have my authority respected—that is all." And Mother, as she puts it, reasonably expects understanding to be enough—without authority. Then, see the daughter, bland, moon-faced, pale, and eyes unfocused, as unexpressive as Rorschach, and you have the same family that I first saw.

Mr. Mace complains that his authority is being undercut by the mother, and the girl invites a battleground. The mirror reflects the mace to her mother, and the mother and the father battle: "How is she to be raised?" as if the "child" were now in her formative years.

The therapist covers by thinking of the legal implications of treating psychosis in his office. If this family gets to him, he wants to scream and run. After the first hour he must decide whether his own life will suffer from the energy loss that must come as he makes contact. In experiencing the rich dynamics unfolding as the family, through its efforts in his presence over several years, step by step becomes aware by changing its behavior, the therapist reexperiences the struggles in his first year of life. Early struggles are reenacted in his office.

As always, the therapist must be one step freer than his patient of the conflict.

As you will notice in these descriptions, it is the reinforcement toward dysfunction that has been emphasized. The therapist's task is to reduce by bringing into awareness those feedback fields that trip the family predicament toward more intense disturbances. Early struggles must be contexted by awareness of present-day strengths.

The symptom, then, is not viewed as an end product or as a by-product, but rather as a cause of the symptom: the Mace family's isolation can cause more isolation, and even the therapist wants to turn away. The effort to deny the state of aloneness may serve to alienate those who might give friendship.

To illustrate in a simple manner: the woman who is to become a geriatric psychologically withdrawn person receives a telephone call in her apartment from a cousin. Her isolation is already so intense that she responds to the hello with tears, "No one visits me." Whining angrily, "You didn't call before." The visiting cousin is less likely to call again. Loneliness can cause loneliness, and symptoms may be the cause of symptoms.

The wielding of the Mace family's weapons made necessary—in self-protection—these weapons. The problems of disarmament and the arms race in a family are not unlike those faced by nations. As soon as Father Mace put down his club, Mother squirted his defenselessness, and Daughter, mirroring his need for justice, villainously reminded him that he has displaced the club to an underground position. Father, so attacked, verified the accusation by clubbing. This is how, over time, the substance of a dream is realized. How could such misfortune befall a family?

The therapist's problem is to help the family become aware of the vicious cycle in which it is caught and the reinforcement procedures that trigger the same cycle on its next round. He must discover how to strike when the matches are damp, so that his action does not increase the conflagration uselessly or blow the family or one of its members into the hospital. Catching the point where one can approach the conflict requires the skill of a labor-management negotiator who, with a small dry comment, can pinpoint the one small area triggering out of dynamic deadlock.

Sometimes the therapist operates as a jujitsu expert, relating to the family by using the weight of their conflict to unmask them. He may knowingly play a characteristic family role, not for the purpose of fooling anybody, but rather to make an action interpretation to demonstrate experimentally how by saying the magic words he can cause the usual expectation. His carefully maintained incongruity holds his position workable. He may use his behavior to clarify the predicament by actively denying that the predicament exists, until a family member, as the representative of the family group, must inform him of its rules. If he wishes to be related to the family, he must make available at least a small part of himself to their game.

Absurdity is a powerful instrument. It may be the only way to break the all-encompassing spiral system that sweeps like a tornado. If the therapist joins the tornado, he may be left debris. If he moves out of relationship, he may end up debris. He may persist in the swirl by making comments that are not even tangentially related to the family system. He stands outside their system but focuses relationship on his absurd presence.

"What did you have for breakfast?" he interrupts an out-of-contact quarrel, which has set tornado warnings. The Maces are going into battle. "And how many minutes did you cook your eggs?"—this sets perspective against which the rising tornado swirls back to the horizon. As he does not engage in the family's system, but also does not stay out of relationship, the therapist is in what, to the family, is a very novel position—and therefore an uncertain one.

The same communication problems exaggerated in the Mace family exist as part of every family's system. Though the vicious cycles do not build to such a pitch, becoming locked into step is a problem for even the more ordinary family.

A family's clipped, measured words, metronomed by Father and then by Mother, can catch the therapist-listener in the rhythm and in the antirhythm. But the child who slips and skids out of the metronome's reach and is called delinquent will soon stop coming or prevent therapy if the therapist is caught in the rhythmic pacing and thereby cannot understand the child's need to make his own music.

The parent will find no reason to be there if the therapist takes the antimetronome position. They have already had excellent advice they cannot take.

The therapist's clarification of the family conflict may be as simple as his beating time with one hand on arm of chair and, when asked about it, saying, "I am trying to catch the family rhythm. Each family has a pace, you know. I think your son will have a different pace in his family—I wonder about your grandchildren. It must be useful in your business to be tuned in to detail."

Father states proudly: "I guess I am exacting. I learned that while flying with my crew over Berlin. My men trusted me, and with attention to detail we stayed alive. Many others went down."

The therapist responds with twinkling amusement: "Then I can understand why you insist that your son cut the grass without missing a blade. Was the family you grew up in that way when you were growing up?"

Three generations of family are held in focus.

Mother answers: "His father was a failure." She is trying to get off the hook herself and avoid the family problem.

The therapist responds: "When your family got started—when you were courting—was exactness something you admired in each other?"

The slippery boy is amused by this conversation as it builds: the metronome is being discussed as something that exists rather than as something within himself that attacks him as careless and threatening to world security. He is less depressed by his own self-criticism.

Power structure is important to the bomber's family, but the obsessive rituals overlay more richness of contact than the manual of organization makes apparent. Family conflicts have become internal, and there is less need than with the Maces to build the family out of vulnerable conflicts buried deep within each person's makeup.

The bomber's family is only apparently closed. There is just one way to run a bomber and the captain is the captain and any deviation from rules is set down as insurrection, but aside from the declared rules they are a softhearted crew. A family machine so organized is ideal for emory-dust operations. Though one son leads the scout troop through their eagle paces, extending the machine a generation, the slithery one, biologically less capable—so his mother says—of infant feeding by the clock, is still out of step. For this poet son, metronomed exactness is a joy to sabotage, and this has become his way of being at one with his family. Mother wisely is trying to sneak him out the back door.

Mother, as copilot, having chosen her pilot husband, looks

for individuality by identifying with a son's rebelliousness. And Father likewise is able to pursue his warlike course only as long as there is a son to war with—to make his organization meaningful he needs something to organize against!

The therapist dedicated to changing this family style of living will probably fail. But if instead he is dedicated to building an increased capacity to understand and handle this style of living successfully, he is likely to succeed, to make possible the change that makes a difference. The parents, toward the end of therapy, realized that the "delinquent" son could not use the particular kind of nourishment they had to offer. A boarding school without animosity was their way of coping, and the copilot, instead of looking for personal freedom through identifying with her son, turned to individual therapy.

Once a family has achieved more contact with the functioning of its own operating systems, it will by definition function as a place of better reality testing. This improves the climate within which the individual family members can create themselves. Old conflicts and misperceptions, long reinforced or made reasonable by being matched by those of others, now seem irrational, and family therapy may be followed by a wish for individual work. As long as one family member can use another to deny his inner conflict, there is reduced opportunity for self-examination—the other's problems form such marvelous excuses. Whether to proceed with technical assistance becomes the choice of the individual. But the lines of communication within the family have been opened.

In a family the sharing of painful loss and of pleasure— the privately significant experiences—gives meaning to the relationship. But more than that, it helps each person to be

73

aware of the special problems—the special coding and decoding—the special distortions—that the other has been schooled to engage in.

The idiosyncrasies of upbringing tend to be reinforced by inducing repetition from within the family. This is less likely to occur when the distortion is knowingly decoded.

We do not often acknowledge the happy capacity of the chosen happenstance environment to reinforce capacity rather than disability, or the need for each of us to enhance ourselves by skillful choice of a potentiating environment. A school program may so operate that its style reinforces into progressively worsening difficulty children whose behavior in another school would be highly valued, catalyzing the growth of self-reinforcing systems. Creativity may be penalized, the child-written *avant-garde* poem held up for ridicule. Tail-wagging smilingness may be considered either stupidity, lack of gumption, or strength of character, depending on the culture of the school.

In the family, it is the matching of individual styles to each other that sets the reinforcement and alters what grows. The reinforcement of a family style may be further reinforced by the style of the neighborhood, which has been chosen by intention or by the circumstances that have brought about or befallen the family unit. In certain social milieus, the growth of capacities are valued, if not explicitly, then implicitly and by behavioral response. The child who is not a thief in a thieving neighborhood has no way to expand beyond the family's limitation through relationship to peers or the police. The therapist-observer must be aware of the breadth or narrowness of the family's reinforcement system.

the
ingredients
of family

IN BETWEEN THE WORDS of the stories so far, experience has been building. This song has been a way of telling about what I have observed. The juncture points and phasings, my points of contact with what has happened, have rhythm within them. Now I shall try to be more open.

A family begins at its first culmination point, the marriage.

Each marriage is the birth of a new family.

The courtship is the gestation time—often abortive.

Each new family is derived from two older families. (Single families rarely cross-pollinate except in hill country.) The offshoots of two old families unite to form a new family, cross-pollinate and germinate tissue for another. Two old families send offshoots, each of which includes trained-in systems for maintaining the character that was originally structured into it. Advancement, education, psychoanalysis, poverty, and illness change the offshoot so that it may be unrecognizable as part of the old family. The offshoots of two old families form a new one. Rapidly changing background—a new syntax—means that there must be change to stay the same. Standing still means changing without regard to context.

As the wind blows the pollen through the air, it becomes carried by its own weight or lack of it—higher or lower, farther or beyond. Some pollen travels many miles, depending on wind conditions. Some pollen requires a lower life form, an insect carrier. The offshoot of each family may be carried to the next town or Chicago or across the ocean, depending upon whether the Army is recruiting, or whether a stewardess' job becomes available, or whether the factory in town to avoid a union encourages migration. Happenstance is not to be denied.

One family may produce different weights in offspring. The happenstance circumstances, which each offspring contacts, make the different kinds of offshoots much more different.

The selective process in the human species is not so different from that among other mammals—there is no mathematical formula as yet with which to plot the marriage of calculating machines or people. At the either-or points of nocturnal moment's hesitation, a slight variation, a decision may be changed as a new contrast is seen while looking backward to remember the night before. A new moment's input may set the correction control system toward a new forward trend. The future, as it happens, reorganizes the patterns of the past.

The marriage of two calculating machines under the supervision of an engineer or a physicist can now be supervised so that the machines may be matched to produce a desirable union—desirable from the engineer's point of view. Two cells of a political party contacting each other may combine to form a new organism that is particularly vital, or one so balanced as to be unable to go beyond to another generation.

Two offshoots of two families, a knight and his beloved, may form a union that is encrusted in armor and enriches nothing.

But the word "enriches" implies some purpose.

Animal breeders have become expert at combining the offshoots of two strains so as to produce more beef or more milk or a variety more highly resistant to disease. There are as yet no consultants for men except some military films.

The lonely young soldier may carry with him a purpose for his marriage as disconnected from family tradition as can be, but he carries with him in the movement of his cells the chromosomal DNA structure out of which he grew.

His beloved likewise has structured into her a style and purpose that filter her basic metabolism into a choice mechanism. This sets control by ruling out certain kinds of males as being inconceivable. But then they may be thrown together by a circumstance in a foxhole.

The tradition of purposefulness is a part of the human communication system, but it is the unintentional messages, those bits of correction after the decision has been made, that come out as the statement of a bachelor friend: "She feels right." And this unrandom choice determines the union of two old families. This is not to undermine the need for road maps—but road maps never fashioned steering systems. And the family *has* built in a steering system, which holds it on trajectory as it generates a future nonexistent in the past.

The previous chapters have built up the concept of behavioral psychology and the idea that innate processes have a characteristic path for a single species. My stories have worked to lift this path in the human species into awareness for technical discussion. For me, a theory of the human family should be built on a framework that is useful in comparative description of family life in other species too.

Recent studies of other mammals indicate that each species has its own family structure. This tradition is maintained by the self-correction which we call natural selection. It is an aspect of the species' physiological-behavioral-anatomic daily evolution.

This is not to say that birds from New York decide that migration to Miami will enhance their protective coloring or avoid the windswept snows, but rather that those birds which adopt this pattern of behavior survive and are available to pass on by one means or another this behavior to the next generation. The human species would not survive if it did not have ways of reinforcing behaviors that reproduce and facilitate the programming of the young so they can communicate with the previous generation and be taught to cope with traditional problems. These problems link each generation to the next.

Over the long term, these links are self-generative, setting out the problems, their solutions, and the structure to be followed.

This same issue may be seen from an evolutionary view.

And new problems do arise by sudden spurts or decline, ebb and flow, in whooping cranes and man. Population explosion, like too much rainfall, is not easily controlled. Control of reproduction may be reached. The control, unlike the problem, will not easily be set into neutral statistics. To control population we move in close to home.

The reinforcement and decay and the control operations of natural selection do apply to behavior in the day-to-day process.

Natural selection during population explosion can apply to the encouragement of certain kinds of characters that can survive in closer quarters. How do such new kinds of characters develop? Marriage is no averaging process, nor multiplication. The mixture of two old pieces of furniture, when set in the context of a new low-ceilinged room or a split-level house, may bring an effect so unlike the traditional statement of the old family home that it is strange to be reminded that little Jojo could be the offspring of his parents. Indeed, it may be strange to realize that the type of family that Jojo's parents have created seems to bear no resemblance to their creators. Older Jojo does not like to rattle around his grandparents' big drafty house.

Where is behavioral transmission between the generations?

Each family's characteristics are set by one partner against the background of the other. Each such change alters the whole picture and creates new choices to be made *never* known before. New unknowns become apparent as we expand into the future. Or two hardened conflicts may marry, and each, being a counterpoint to the other, so reinforce the area of problem that they wall out what else is opening up in the new generation. Offspring not changing with the times caricature the old system—a slow motion-picture in a modern theatre. If a single characteristic becomes highly accentuated, the family organism may, or may not, be enhanced in its generative capacity.

As there is a movement toward those characteristics that are less common, extreme enhancement or extreme diminution of capacity to pursue the ordinary pattern of selection may occur. Unusual people often feel this pinch when they are looking for a mate. This is to be expected. As a particular cell is less in phase with a thousand, its survival potential is altered. For groups of ten thousand develop institutions that may alter the chance of finding each other for those who live near the edges of the normal distribution curve. This language is applicable to experimental studies with other species as well as our own.

It is the ecologists who have developed techniques of discussing biological systems on a square foot of land or a single field or an island. This is not just a count of onions by their number, but an awareness of the tears they create, and of the stumbling fingers cutting onions giving up the cutting to wipe the eyes. And there are many such cycles on our growing cubic foot of land. The rigors of the weather, the fertility of the soil, the rainfall, the aeration of the soil by worms, and the need for aeration of the plants and the succulents for the herbivores and the succulence of the herbivores for meat-eaters, and the whole continuity is a field that includes the human species even as he counts himself as the outside observer as if the world were a creation of his logic. *Tyrannosaurus rex* fell into the same mud puddle. The cycle did go on without him.

The continuity must be broken down to build a net of theory to discover new ways of building new nets. One net has been weaving since I began this book. Weaving sometimes deftly or more crudely, the question is simply: Will new data be created?

If a farmer can only sow enough seed to obtain more seed than he has sown, he is ready to proceed. There is a gradient necessary to prevent the dying out of a new idea or a people. This has nothing to do with human purposes or human pleasure: people make a purpose of their natural progression. Their symbolized purpose is a retrospective viewpoint of the past.

Some people would confine the breeding process necessary for human survival to evening hours, and some would eliminate chance and make all sexual activity undebatable. The unthought-about structure—the sexual cadence of our music and dance—is more clearly seen in the ritual of the primitive fire dance or on valentines. These biological behaviors are highly structural.

The more basic, the more formal. The built-in process catalyzes energies toward a less random choice. The commonest behaviors are protected from social change by being more private. The secrets of the analyst's couch are the most common acts.

Two poor fish mate while they are sucking on weeds and after having received a potion called Martini. They have ridden across the plains many moons to return to a tribal gathering place and will fulfill a betrothal made before they were born by tribal union.

There are those who describe the ritual rites of intercourse or sneezing, childbearing or child-rearing, as something that somebody did to somebody, rather than as two people influencing each other in a crescendo of anatomy emotion, action sweating all as one. A cat must sneeze just like a queen with a tickle in her nose.

A glance between two people, between a husband and wife, a father and his son, can never be written down as it exists. But the crescendo of experience, the glance breeding itself, has a meaning very different from what two people looked at each other. And so it is with the family. With our new language, we can share the growing to and from movement of crescendo as the moment builds its cycles.

The waxing-waning rhythm of a child inside the mother may so upset her rhythm that she stops eating, and the soup he lives in is changed. I think the baby is sending messages by his kicks, though not by intention. And this language is more liable to cross systems than the subject-predicate language of who-done-what-to-which.

The intercourse between characteristics of two people waxes and wanes without intentional reason. The rhythm of the internal clock, the 28-day cycle, man's crescendo of sexual interest—these psychophysiological experiences have been abstracted over time into thoughts and words and social structures. The persistence of the structure of our laws is determined by being congruent with the cycles of the people. Out-of-contact cultures do not persist.

Each family has its pulse.

The family pulse can be described in terms of change in pace—its change in volume and its space, its soul-searching. A child's cut nails do not as easily experience picking up pins: but reduced opportunity for fine movements of the fingers—a feature of our species—may make scratching sister more entertaining, and the nails are cut shorter. A theory of the family includes the feedback between behavioral-biological-psychophysiological-anatomical mechanisms, which are all names used to arrange the National Library of Medicine into different sections. Fancy words such as "feedback process" deny their own simpleness. Think of intercourse, and one becomes aware that two people act on each other in a manner far more exquisitely human than any abstract anatomical or even musical language could ever express. Sex is not a who-done-what-to-which except in the special case of rape. Man's linear apparatus may have given rise to his linear thinking, but his straightforward statement is inconsequential unless received in a manner that gives it meaning. Man is received by woman, which may enhance them to an orgastic climax. But their union encompasses an infinite series of contexts.

The home that a family selects may enhance its noise, its solemnity, or its fun. It is an instrument of the family's unintentional utilization of props for the building of its own way of life. And the choice of home, limited by the building code of an area, may set limits upon the possible. It may program the children so they will carry those building codes to the next generation as a base for deviation. And physiological building codes are set by acoustics of the house. Will the call of the children in the night be loud or soft? Will the room resonate to high or low pitches? High- or low-pitched demands get different responses, as every radio advertiser knows. The influence of the children on the parents' sexual life may also be determined by building codes.

A house differently shaped means a differently shaped

family, and a family theory must include an awareness of props, perhaps mud and thatch. The plenitude of small sticks may be important to the nesting of small birds. If cellophane is more available, they use it, and ladies admire their taste in colors. The mating of deer depends upon the supply of grass, leaves, and certain species of bark. The nesting habits of mice, if interfered with by too large a mouse population, disorganizes nesting and reduces population. Most animals have a certain amount of territory that is necessary for their life process. Too much crowding or too little proximity alters the creation of new generations. Territory is not just for food gathering: it is structured by habits and signal-sending and receiving and the need to keep waste in balance with new food. This story can be elaborated and enriched by animal biologists and botanists. But the social structure of a pack of wolves is not unlike our own. The animal observers are amazed at the elaborate rituals of the animal kingdom. Have they been taught by us? Or did Noah do the job to while away his forty days and nights?

An enzyme that is produced at a time when there is no substrate, like an oven that heats only when there is no cake, disrupts the generative process. A wolf who is sexually aroused only when he has made his girl friend angry may remain a bachelor. But if he meets one who is like him, and their daughter is matched in the next generation by a husband soft and mellowed, this daughter may seem very loud. Modern painting, viewed in the context of an Aztec temple, is exceedingly beautiful. But placed on the same wall with a Victorian seascape, it becomes like a shooting wife matched to a prissy father-husband. Mating is a form of matching, and the family encompasses the enhancements that arise from the mating. Every artist knows that two sides of a single event may move in the context of each other to transcendent heights. A theory of the family must find a means of focusing on and symbolizing this process.

Our theoretical model must allow us to talk technically of intercourse as the model of a field of action. Enhancement can be measured in terms of rhythm, vigor of activity, amplitude of oscillation, sounds, and sweatings. But though these are scientific measurements reflecting for a given duration the enhancement that has taken place, still, dynamically, they do not represent the growth-progression process.

Technical formulation of what has been just natural— process at the growth edge of change—is the problem of our generation.

If it were enough to say that the enhancement that occurs is natural or divine, then the student's technical question— "Why do volcanoes erupt at a particular time?" could be answered with "Because it is natural." And perhaps man never would have discovered the relationship between intercourse and having children: once both were simply considered natural. In some primitive tribes today this relationship is not defined.

The oscillation in intercourse, the enhancement to climax, seems to be as common to mammals as the process of feeding the young with breast milk. To biologists this characteristic of mammals is a factor that defines the group. The comparative study of such behavior from one species to the next within the class mammals might assist in our attempt to build a way of simulating in a model family process.

Study of comparative behavior from one species to the next has been found to show progressions that relate the various species in a very useful way. The study of humans within the context of a general biological theory will allow us to see the new dimensions in mating, childbearing, and child-rearing practices. The crap-playing gambler uses dice differently from the man whose decision rests on a single throw. The lucky gambler on the long haul is said to know the odds and bets them. This scientific study is to some gamblers automatic. The behavior of man and of other creatures has over the long term survived him. But this is looking back.

A new branch of science studying preservation of our species is no longer inappropriate.

Do we have a science of generations moving forward? There is a limit to predictions from the past. They cannot encompass an awareness of the momentary target and the control-system process that selects that information being used as corrective information.

The anthropologist watching a Blackfoot Indian's afternoon may give long explanations of how the rain dance originated. He is an observer who looks backward, and the chief who remembers is also looking back. But the foot dancing knows only when its step is wrong and corrects it. Did the Minoans of Crete prepare their garbage heaps for archaeologists to explain? In what way is the grown-up's recollected childhood a function of the growing, forty-pound boy uncontexted by awareness of what weight sixty pounds is like?

And each change in a family changes everything, and the development of one new kind of behavior shifts the context of others, making many obsolete. This shift in the observer's values may be determined by the development of one new prop, something simple like a wheel. The backward view cannot solve the problems of progression.

The family of husband and wife can remain in contact with each other until they are born by their child to a context that is new. The trajectory through this new family way holds its course programmed with patterns built in by selection. The statistical chance of a field expanding over time has set the givens. Two persons are not likely to marry if they cannot send/receive signals that make them significant to each other. The concatenation of their intermeshing proclivities—what they see in each other—may give rise to an expression of pleasure, pain, disruption, destruction, wholesomeness, idiocy, and so on into the long list of value judgments.

It is my value judgment that an animal that perceives as much of what exists around him as is necessary to his unfolding pursuits has an advantage over another creature whose design for living remains more circumspect.

Undoubtedly the swan thinks of man as stupid for needing such a great head and is quite unaware of man's interest in the serpentine quality of the swan's neck. There is little interspecies talk, though the traditions of geese, ducks, and turkeys are known by those breeders who prepare them for the Thanksgiving market. Remember, though, now that supreme humans can unshovel Pompeii and Belsen enshrined in ashes, and can list the advantages of Romans over Huns, turkey historians may someday record the Thanksgiving massacres as passed gobble to gobble by the survivors. To avoid such absurdity, we must accept this simplicity: *being* humans we must extol the virtue and supremacy of our own species—at least for the time being, until we can learn to acknowledge that each species, having its own perceptual system, defines its own kind of world. A police dog gives his master warning when they have learned to talk together. A human baby speaks when he is understood. New concepts of information exchange bring us closer to direct communication with other species.

Humans are better able to understand the communication systems that have developed within their own species than those of other species. This is not surprising and has not been a problem, except in science fiction, when we negotiate with equals who breathe nitrous oxide on other planets. This science-fiction problem stirs humans to be aware that a particular human system of communication is one of many and exists to be studied.

Any study of the communication system within the family must include the bridging of the gap between the different behavioral psychology of the three main subgroups within our species—male, female, and child.

Men are more intrinsically different from women than any man will ever understand, and the obverse applies symmetrically. How then do these two creatures tune in on each other? A man's touch resting on the skin of his female partner receives information from the skin he touches with. But the person touched has made contact too, for this touch is two persons. What the other one experiences is revealed by the warmth in a thousand cues, which have been programmed into the child by training. This training is as traditional as the courting behavior that anyone can watch in a suburban fish tank or a zoo.

Humans courting grunt at each other in a series of infant flips, cries, and wails refined between baby time and courting time into the sex language of Chinese or French. The courting rituals are laid pattern on pattern, conditioning the tendrils of a time-delayed DNA coding. Cooing and billing are more traditional than most people know, though techniques are refined with each new discovery.

The sniffing of dogs communicates as does their smell, and their barkings can drown out the vocalization of a hungry child. Fledgling parents-in-process, fresh from their eggs, open their mouths to give the signal for a worm. Communication is a language—words are one form.

To humans, the vocal system has been refined in a way we all admire, and our nest-building function likewise has advanced over the thousand years from the cliff-dwelling temples of our ancestors. Fire, the wheel, and atomic energy give us a sense of pride in a job of survival well done. But is our grammar keeping pace? Subject-predicate reasoning—cause and effect—Aristotle's fable that the essence is the thing—all have become a special case in a broader view of our modern science. But our grammer is unchanged. We are losing language contact with our tools. The family is the subgroup within the culture where blond and curly learning machines are built. I wonder how it happens? Can we learn by variations?

One cannot speak of the family as a single unit without relating it to the context of a culture. This cultural assemblage carries forward through the newness another generation's experience from the past. Each culture has its own particular kind of family, with its own techniques for teaching infants to learn. This perpetuates its kind. Each culture is built of many individuals who, with banns announced or undeclared, follow the same biological rituals to advance the functions of a family. They talk about their history in different ways.

A single family may reproduce and enhance a tradition that weighs against the purpose of its community. These families provide the unexpected possibilities that help the community create its changings. Such crazy families may produce creative children, who transform what was once crazy into a new mode of living. These same families may enhance bizarreness in the direction of disruptive disorganization.

No family is a miniature edition of the stereotype for a thousand. The offshoot of a thousand families is not an average, for who would know how to average families, each of which is so different from the next? An average human family with six legs, six arms, and an appropriate aggregate of heads cannot be put together into a family conference, cannot join with the elders of the tribe to negotiate a dowry.

Each family is very different from the next. No two people are alike and no two families are alike. It is difficult to find useful themes with which to structure the sameness and difference of each family. The sameness has been discussed primarily in terms of our common humanness. Our sameness soon moves beyond our words, and yet it is this invisible matrix that we must understand in order to persist.

Families have been traditionally grouped in terms of their possessions. This has been the only way of describing the family's growth and decay. This kind of description appears in the IQ test where the child's acquisition of knowledge as possession is used to represent his learning process. Theories built from possession-conscious descriptions do not reflect the basic human process of learning and of "familying." It is only as we can define process and styles of evolving that we can build a theory useful for changing the family (*and* perhaps its possessions).

Child-rearing, in spite of variation, is more alike among humans than it is different. Our mouths and tongues and ears and feet are made the same. And budding too is very similar among vastly different trees. Trees reproduce more like trees than like birds. The variation among humans in their child-rearing practices is never so great as between the human species and other species. That humans are more human than otherwise is a matter so exceedingly obvious as to be forgotten. Intraspecies manners consider making our own skin into purses a very special crime. Most species have ways of teaching manners that are ritualized survival techniques to protect their own kind.

Child-rearing practices are used in this context to include the child's teaching the parents from his earliest moment of life those needs which are to be attended to *now*. Even the growing infant in the womb is not an inert creature. Each infant human communicates to a pretuned receptive organ mother about his needs. This communication may be an open mouth whose configuration neatly fits the ready breast full of milk. Enzyme and substrate, wailing mouth, hungry to take in, and breast full to giving out, together form a nursing system. The child's activity, his falling asleep, the mother's relaxation, her muscle tone in relation to his, the skin warmth between two—all are messages, intermeshing exchanges, that have to do with the maintenance of life.

Child and mother contact as their receptors are delicately entwined. The child's and mother's needs are more effectively communicated when they receive adequate perception. They must learn to share some coding. The crude circuits are already built in. A snipped-across baby-to-placenta telephone cord begins the first breath and a broader-channeled message-exchange system. Letter-writing comes much later. The persons who support the mother-child relationship are very often husbands, though in some societies they are grandmothers or aunts. A supporting person during the early child-rearing progression is necessary. By "necessary" I simply mean that such a three or more unit, at least for our species, is more likely to propagate into further such units.

Now a grandfather who has a grandchild come into his family has a different kind of life. And with each such exchange all members change.

A husband watching his child being mothered remembers being mothered himself. The child's unique method of addressing his mother and the matching they begin set a contrast that informs the father that his wife is different from the mother he recalls. And the father's support of the mother while she is mothering the child reactivates old patterns usefully built in for another epoch. These may enhance or interfere with the mother-child process. Each epoch, past and future, has its resonating circuits, which remain to affect our every moment.

Where is the beginning of the family? In the mating season? Which comes first, the chicken or the egg?

A child's family spirals over time with his own family later on. And conventions like beginning-middle-end, like north-south-east-west, are the traditional ways of structuring our language. This code is less than useful for our purpose of measuring the cycle as it grows. Is there a beginning and end of the child's hunger—or does sleepiness take over? And not long ago the drugstore alarm clock was used to set a beginning and an end to child and mother's rhythm.

But the child's capacity to receive from the mother that which is necessary at a particular moment in order to live requires that the mother be able to listen to the child: to experience him in terms of her knowledge of the child outside of herself. This capacity depends upon her own background as a child. The generations mix up that way.

One generation cannot be too different from the next or communication will not work. They were all very similar until recently when the new mathematics turned the spiral faster.

When the father was seducing his new wife and having child with her, he depended upon touch to know how best to do it. This improves the odds of having babies. Being in touch gives him knowledge of what it must be like even though her system is so different from his. And the wife's touch of husband depends upon knowing that he is differently built; her touch of him will be experienced within his system, which her perceptors cannot report. He speaks by his response. And so it is with a mother and her child. A father cannot have the experience of nursing his child, but must learn how his wife experiences in relation to the child by what she communicates to him. And this communication is not in ideas but in cellular response—soft eyes and glowing skin.

A baby doll, a mother doll, and a father doll are what would be if everything were as the baby-raising books that everybody reads say it should be. To make this all more than an idea, to feel the joy of sparkling eyes thrilling to the limbs, and to sleep quietly requires the soft language of body memories more intrinsic than words.

But each child playing with her doll is playing like a kitten jumping on a mousy something when there is no mouse that is small enough for her to catch. Now the father's knowledge of his wife's experiences of mothering, and how they change her being a wife to him in a little particular way, is important. For that knowledge allows him to correct and maintain the system: he becomes a different kind of husband to her so the two may continue to have a kind of rewarding experience similar to the one that brought about the child's birth.

But all this exchange of information is not what anybody has said. The baby who sends his information, often softly resting in his diaper, tells thereby about the problems of his food intake. The mother's milk flow may give returning information about the kind of experience that is coming into her endocrine gland. The communication is more sugar or less, and different kinds of milk. This is not an over-the-counter transaction. Whether the baby holds his hands on the bottle with exploring feeling or with jangled rhythm changes the responsive pattern set up in the mother. She feels structured with meaning by the child's little hands. And father's rhythm may reflect a biology that has not become attuned to the idea of parenthood.

And this kind of experience is communicated to the younger or older brothers or sisters as they come into the nursery. And how much each person is allowed to experience each other, directly or mediated by a third, is a highly variable matter. To a listening brother the infant baby's wail may bring red waves of anger, green envy, or the purple wish to scream. His physiology changes. Excitement may build a spontaneous fire, burning underground or flaring in red ears.

Just as the position of the mother's arms, eyes, breasts, and body is constant for the species, though with considerable variation, so it is that human exchanges are determined by what body experience is like. Man's body experiences differently when smaller and crawling or larger and toddling. The nerves that are not fully developed when he is born may never become as fully developed as his brother's. Maturing is a function of the child's feeding-sleeping-action pattern, which activates the nervous tissue growth, and so the circle spirals through time.

It is not possible for a toddler to run the way a grown-up does. His legs and balance are different. The father and the mother went through the stages that are usual for all human infants. Each child, in his own time, is programmed by his body's experience, which changes the way he grows up and learns to use his body. The programming in his body may be different from what he tells as he maps experience into words. Parents have grown through the period of being the infant child, being remembered as infants, or experiencing their siblings in different ways. What they think or have read or been taught about being parents, matched to the way they were actually programmed, sets their course of action. Two different parents programmed differently must act very differently to send the same message to their child.

The mother knows that she must minister to the child, using her own ways of decoding the signals he sends into information that will govern her response.

The child-in-the-mother is an image that is like a book for decoding the messages the new child sends; it is necessary for the new child to send messages that the mother can decode according to her book. And the family members code each other, and the child joins in the information system long before he is born.

The vigorous child will be considered hyperactive by the vigorous mother whose own movement has been criticized and pained into becoming highly restrictive. Or trouble may begin because the two rhythms match in some troublesome way. They may swing like a bridge in the wind unless dampened by a third. These rhythms are time elements of information exchange.

But the father who can reassure the mother by taking over some of the activity of their child may be able to make between child and mother a more comfortable gentle muscle togetherness. Another father, rejecting them both, being unaware of either, may set them together so that they will act corded and bathed together—a baby plastered against the uterine walls. Although former navel channels of endocrine communications are directly blocked after birth, a sigh, a breath, a drooping hand, a gut smell, or a rumble may use belly-button paths. And mother's feeling that "His hunger gets to me inside my skin" is no mere allusion. When the child is very young, such primitive communication allows a gradual transition between the inside and outside world.

The capacity of the family unit to signal from one pseudopod to another is necessary to concerted action in a detailed manner that fits the species pattern. This pattern requires traditional props, which are also information. To survive in winter country, a lair warm enough for survival extends the womb. And the Neanderthal brings back food for those who remain at home. He nuzzles the little ones, who, unlike the smaller baboons, are unable to cling to their mother's hair while the troop proceeds in its tour of hunting grounds.

Our evolving capacity to communicate and to pool information makes our species more fit for survival.

You may ask me at this point why I have not reduced this theory to a formula that can be placed on a blackboard. The answer is very simple. I am not able.

The problem of communication or information exchange has been selected as the central spiral on which our information is being hung. A fundamental observation is that we lose information as we organize anything. The lost information drops out completely because it has no place in our system, and such loss increases the more neatly we arrange a particular set. To a grown-up's system, the child's system is less organized. Or is it just a different system to be linked by time progression into proximity with ours?

An infant child is capable of screaming and does scream, as even older children do in all sorts of other sounds. Sounds made as he draws in air, sounds made as air is let out. There are sounds of the glottis, sounds of the nose, sounds of the chest, clicking and whirrings and wonderful sounds with which it is almost impossible for any adult to communicate. But no adult has exactly the same kind of throat that a child has. Yet we have learned how to teach children particular ways of selecting, from all the possible sounds that they can make, certain kinds of sound that will become important as a communication to us.

Now, the Chinese child can use but one range of phonetics, and the Bantu uses clicks. But all these sounds are more distinctly human than either a cat or a seagull or a gifted bird could ever imitate. Within the range of human sounds, of human rhythms or the sounds of the particular configuration of the throat that humans have, there is great selecting out as a single set is found. And certain sounds will probably never be uttered by any kinds of humans except infants. Just as mouth and throat and chest movements alter breathing into infant sounds, the same and other infant movements become received as movement language.

And the child's movements each receive a response of movement, which within our own traditions are often not considered. No one pays attention to how cute Mother is as she is seen by her child. There is so much research to be done.

Gravity-plus-props also trains children.

The bed moves as the child shifts his weight, and the way it moves in response to the child's movements depends upon the kind of bed that it is—a mat or a pallet of eucalyptus leaves. The child's experience with his own movements depends upon the experience of things that his movements come into conjunction with, which are to him a part of his movements. Surely the infant does not entertain our who-done-what-to-which conventions?

And swaddling clothes give different kinds of movements to the child's movement than does being strapped to a board or being jostled in a baby carriage with cheaper or more expensive springs. And these kinds of movements responding to the child's movements are information in terms of how his field of movement feels. They are experienced as one long before they are broken into particles for the purpose of being named.

The movement of a father tired from the office and told to pick up the kid trains the kid's experience of movement differently from the movement of a mother.

And the baby's movements are responded to by the mother and father each in terms of a scanning expectation. This organized frame for understanding what may be the child's random behavior in fact organizes the child's behavior as it structures the parents' responses. Mother's expectation of Father will likewise organize her response to his behavior. Her response, the look of response while he is speaking, guides him as to whether he is getting through to his objective. As he is sending, he receives this return and corrects the coding he is using toward sending more exactly the message he intends. Who can speak exactly to a silent wife—or one who does not listen? There develops a field of expectation that sets and predicts which channel works the best and when the message will sink in. And a prediction made long ago may become a prejudice, restricting discovery and growth.

So it is with children. Their random behavior becomes gradually less random and more congruent with translations that were set by hopes and expectations of what the child should be. In truth, the child never was random, but his system of organizing himself has at first no structure for adults. The human child is limited to the sounds, movements, and energy exchanges instinctive to the species. Were these really random and not set in message units, a mother's milk would not flow in response to his crying.

Gradually a refinement sets upon this broader field of

ways of being, and this rules out more and more potentials by which humans can organize. But abstraction requires information loss. As this organizing grows by conventional selection into action language, verbal language, and the many "natural" ways of being, the growing list of conceivables is entered into a family dictionary. And the sharing of this coding allows a glance to mean so much and is called the closeness of a family.

information
exchange

THE FAMILY IS the primal group in which *learning how to learn* begins. The child is taught how to learn before anybody is aware of teaching, and the learning of the child how to learn teaches the parents how to teach as well. And all this occurs long before the child has ever learned the word "why?" And this nonsequential experience is biologically important. We need to learn new ways of learning, of developing our senses to take in new information. The old information we can leave to the machines.

The animal that perceives as much as possible of what exists around him, and can discard by choice what is of no interest to him, has in this capacity for choice an advantage over other creatures whose design for living remains more circumspect. This is the value system I propose.

Then a family that teaches contact with what exists within it and around it and outside it—and thus acknowledges the larger field of choice—broadens its field of growth by teaching discovery. And some are caught in a restrictive time. Omitting space-time passage they cling to stable images of yesterday's action as if it were now. They are robbed of action contact with what in a moment can become only symbols for tomorrow's recollection. And time spirals by as if untouched by human hands. The word "apple" never rots.

The family that mothers the child exquisitely may not be able to allow the same child to leave off being mothered. Then that family may become one that is more involved with mothering than with mating. And infanting or mothering continue timelessly without the contact that new muscle circuits or weight gain can make. Child-rearing is a noisy in-the-mind affair. Old messages naggingly repeated lose information value.

In the growth from infant to an older kind of animal there is a progression that is true of many different kinds of species. The old dog loses his teeth, and the old man loses his hair, and people as they get older change and getting older is soon a day-to-day affair. For each species the cells change their rate of change to an older kind of tissue in a characteristic way. To date, these changes are named by allusion to astronomical or Greenwich time, base twenty-four hours. And some of the behaviors of the family that were important in the rapid time when the family was younger cease to be important when the family is older. New kinds of circuits, building every day like the new mathematics, build new kinds of problems. And so the family grows with one kind of time as it lives its biological cycles whose rhythms set another kind of time.

Growth in physical dimensions—the sprouting of two breasts or of a larger penis, hair under the arms—is not simply a physical matter. For all humans, the growth of the penis nestled in a new bush of hair means changes. There are new ways of thinking, of experiencing arms and legs, and new smells of body: and in the crescendo reinforcement of all these changes is a new creation not to be dismissed as simply another stage. Such labels stop the action, kill the wing action even as the hummingbird in transit stands still near its nest.

Such crude corrective data as what should be and how, may give no next-move information. The infant child is not taught what he can know, but is fed the ambition to walk long before his legs are strong enough to support him standing up. This is noise in the message system—a message is being sent that cannot be received—the telegraph station for its deciphering and response will open up next week. Or the toddler is expected to be as small as the infant, as cutely remembered as he used to be. And the way children *are* is left to intuition and the hand-me-downs of what we knew before. As we find a language of unfolding—one that does not pretend to stop the action—much new technical study opens out and becomes conceivable.

Growth may be stopped by having no words for progression of legs or arms or hands, or developing of menstruation until one day there is blood. Then, by definition, something began on that day, but what of the progression? Denying this progression till the day of bleeding and using this event to label the progression withholds communication from a changing child. A pubescent child, whatever happens to be her culture, is opening new decoding systems. But if the heralding style changes are unperceived, this narrows her follow-through potential; then the day after, it is as if she had not changed. And one day there is an untimely crisis.

There are certain characteristics usual to the human child as he creates each growth cycle that makes him similar to others creating the same change. But what is common is no limit on creation in spite of expectation.

The epochs of the individual's human development have been studied as individually and sequentially conceived. Where is the language for the as-it-happens process that gives content to these checkpoint namings?

Each physiology has its own language.

Noise and static, energy for jamming, make less available the information useful to guide the contact process.

As the teacher learns techniques of making contact with his students' input system, he gains a perspective. He learns new ways to put out his signals so they will be taken in and decoded as the message he intends. Where is the basic scientific study of this basic human process? How little of our potential as a species do we fulfill? Are there easier ways to accomplish what, implicitly, we expect to be difficult? By our expectation do we make it so? The variation from one family to another, as I have seen them in my office, makes me aware that so far there is no science of learning how to learn. Each family finds in its own simplicities a different way to start. Can we abstract a general system with which to speak about their growth? Can we teach the ways that seem to organize a particular advantage?

The family system operates to inform each other member of what he is like, as seen from a perspective different from the one within which each can see himself. And the individual set has a new interpretation at its borders that feeds the new system enough to make it grow. It grows as it takes in data that it did not create—that did not exist for it before. This growth system operates very differently in different families. Its characteristics are important. The variables usually measured are often irrelevant to the questions we are asking.

A pale skin may to one culture mean illness, and to another anger, and the capacity to contact one's own message-sending from inside is again taught variously in different families: some families continue to consider laziness as tuberculosis, or tuberculosis as laziness. Visiting the doctor is very often calling a consultant to assist the family to contact—to decode the messages sent by a particular family member, or a message sent from the kidney to the bladder without a child's concern. This may become a message to the parents that the child cannot decipher.

In some families where contact is less, the children can be extremely ill before heated brow or lassitude or inability to run is decoded into anything of meaning. Sometimes the person is so sick by the time the message does get through that little can be done. This kind of family is not very useful in terms of its survival.

The doctor who makes contact with his patients values their capacity to communicate body happenings accurately. Long before the most delicate laboratory tests, these happenings may indicate that an effective change of treatment is being made. He must learn to be aware of the variation in the patient's capacity to contact the variation in his sense of well-being. And this kind of contact with oneself is learned very early—in the crib.

Who can hold awareness of constant stimulus unless it be of catastrophic proportion? The process of accommodation to steady states makes the human an excellent instrument for the perception of change. And some families overload their joined inner-sentinel circuits with bowel rumblings, snifflings, and aches, using these to jam communication of ongoing change.

When the family arrives, I see them first through contacting my own shift from the steady state that their arrival has disrupted. I know them by the sense of change that we produce in one another and experience within ourselves. Who can be aware of what is so usual that it is omnipresent? The freshness of each varied unbalance that we sense in our effort at restoration is empathy.

But empathy is not enough. This is the medium that I must use to make the family aware of systems that they have absorbed by gradual drift. And this kind of drift has a propagation that is not usually talked about except in terms of the most out-of-the-ordinary manifestations. And it is these propagations of unconscious propaganda that make the substance of a child's education.

When what is taught without awareness in an automatic style is mixed with what is taught by intention, there begins a creative process yet to be defined. The same intentional behavior will produce a different response in a different kind of child (a difficulty for mental-hygiene programs as they are now conceived).

Whether a child will become a good hunter in the jungle or on Wall Street depends upon his capacity to smell, to hear, and to see sharply the changing quotations or the rustle of a leaf. Some families prosper each other's capacity to be tuned in to the world around them: other families are more involved with maintaining a state of equilibrium unrelated to the curvature of the events of that particular day.

The dog that cannot learn how to cross the street without being hit by a car may be simply that kind of a dog, or the car may be too fast. But the family of which the dog happens to be a member may have unintentionally trained out the patterns and pace specifically designed to that dog's own senses which he might have used to avoid this kind of death.

By training without contact one can train out of a dog what one is trying to train in. It is equally easy unintentionally to train a child to do exactly what one does not wish.

A chosen dog's behavior recalls the adoption family system. A dog, like an adopted child, comes to resemble his adoptive parents. A dog can become neurotic.

Now for the dog this may be because the dog-human exchange system has become disordered: most commonly the family has expected the dog to be a human because he has a human name. This family loses doubly: the dog is not suited to this task, and the master who cannot acknowledge the dog's own skills—his system—can train him only crudely by rote. The dog has a particular sensory system that it is skilled in using. For those less scientifically curious, one can say that making contact with the dog keeps stains off the rugs and keeps him from being killed.

Likewise a family may be more or less able to contact the individuals within it so as to use what each one is like to enhance the growth process.

I believe that increased contact between child and adult will allow an acceleration of teaching now undreamed of. This is the way genius is now created—accidentally. What is now considered normal is simply underdevelopment.

The measurement of contact is important. For this we need new theory. The dog is a symbol with which to form our language. Child- and dog-rearing principles are simple once contact is made.

Some families treat their dogs as if they were a representation of the word "dog" or as if they were a recollection of "dog" yesterday now extended.

This same kind of a family treats one another as if each simply embodied his reputation. There is no awareness of how each experience of an individual at a particular moment is unlike the experience of the day before. This way of not knowing each other goes on day after day, except when they meet occasionally as acknowledged strangers. Like the dog, each family member becomes less able to use his senses in such a way that these will be of value to the whole family. In one such kind of a family, everyone knows in advance what anybody will say all the time. Everybody always says what is expected of him. What will follow the first word is completely predictable, and there seems to be no reason to listen. This can go on for years and years, and everybody reads off the script what he is supposed to be like. Within the family he grows into becoming the actor of that script: the one who on script is supposed to be sick may become sick because the clothes he wears for the part are unrelated to his physiology. He may remain overheated to protect himself from the shivering cold on the script. And this is common and more weird as it happens than I can describe.

Individual members of a particular family, when outside of that family, may be keen observers of their reality. Crossing the threshhold they tune in a new system of reality appraisal. Entering, they wind themselves into a cloistered robe that twists their common sense into a family mythology. As this twisting tightens, the family is a less useful training ground for each member. There is then less opportunity for exchanging with another what each observes to be happening, except as it happened before.

In this particular kind of family the mother and father may see the fuzzing bush of hair, or the increasing size for brassieres, but act as if it were not happening. The girl's age on her birth certificate and her role as the family baby mean no brassieres—regardless. The natural development sequence appropriate to being with enlarging breasts does not receive the response that gives support to creating new kinds of relationships. The fresh, pert acknowledgment of newness may be replaced by full discussions about what kinds of brassieres will someday be safest to buy as if to prevent mother's now evident pendulousness.

There are in each species certain behaviors that come at rutting time. A crescendo of physiological changes comes in rhythmic cycles. Nowadays such cycles are symbolized in endocrine language. Older, less chemical cultures chose equally formalized ways to acknowledge this rhythm. This periodicity may be unrecognized as behavior that extends beyond the uterine wall. When this happens, each person is robbed of capacity to be aware of a kind of information that is useful simply to know about. The technological study of a woman's *total* alternations as she progresses in cycle has only recently been undertaken. The female's periodicity is part of her species behavior, and yet in some families it is denied the respect given to the cycles of the automatic washing machine.

A theory of the family as a biological unit demands attention to human biology and its behavioral manifestations, which includes representation by words. Much has been said by others about words and thoughts and mental representations. These words are not apparently as measurable as the language of substantial time-space energy-mass phenomena that are taking place. Advances in information theory take information exchange into a new dimension. This dimension gathers together words and other language into a theoretical perspective that allows the invention of new kinds of measurement.

The conception that is being presented does not separate thought from behavior and behavior from physiology. Nor does it separate behavior from anatomy or signals from their carriers.

Must life process be studied like a reconstruction of dead boxed tissue?

The way particular family members swing their arms as they walk toward the house may be an important communication that will set the tone of the whole evening more significantly than words uttered as the door is opened. An infant, because of the size and proportion of his body, cannot swing up the walk as his father does. He delightfully caricatures his father's walking. But he is more different from the adult man than any two adult men could ever be.

Each epoch of human development carries with it certain human potentials that may be mobilized in different ways. Adult and child are very different. They have such different cultures. A two-year-old boy in any country may be fascinated with his penis, with a walrus tusk or spear, or with a garden hose. On the other hand, he may be so swaddled in confinement that he can play with nothing. Each experience reinforces a particular selection of what will happen next, but two-year-olds are more like each other than adults can imagine. This may be obvious, but it has important consequences less readily apparent.

The organization of the world around anybody depends upon the apparatus with which he sees it. Imagine the world of a cyclops, or a bug, or an infant, or a man. Consider the size effect on bug and man and baby. Move between that which is defined by size, rate of change in size, placement of sense organs, and think of how much is defined by the training of those arrangements as they vary with age from year to year. Wonder at the apparent constancy of a particular anatomical culture and the intricacy of communicating between these different growth systems. It is amazing that child and parent, menstrual adolescent and grandparent communicate at all. Realizing the need to bridge such difference for common survival action, you will experience the more elemental problem of communication. And learning to communicate between the species is a model for improving our conversations with the little human beasties without pretending that they are just the way we remember ourselves to have been.

A child *to himself* is complete as he moves forward through any single moment. The difference in point of view, experiencing forward versus remembering backward, means a problem of coding information to cross this gap in either direction.

To approach this problem we must take the broader meaning of the concept of communication. Information exchange or communication cannot be usefully limited to verbal exchange which can be printed. A man may receive a communication from a woman which causes his ardor to rise within him without anyone's intention. This woman has intended to look pretty but that is not what attracts him—she walks with a lilt. The man's scanning system seems to locate this particular kind of woman regardless of her presentation, her interest, or any of the messages she intends to send. And each may bypass the other on the street, or, being magnetized together with the slightest excuse they may say "Hello."

Humans translate energy into many forms. These transformations, their continuities and discontinuities, their pace and crescendo are information transmitters. Intention is a small part of the system.

When alarmed, the outermost bird of the flock flies away: the flight of this bird and its pattern disturbs the next bird, and the signal spreads like a rumor, an epidemic, or a chain letter, depending on flock density and signal sending and receiving range.

Is the first bird off the ground the sentinel? This is the traditional question. My kind of question is this: how does one bird's happening to escape an intruder communicate to build an epidemic of response across the flock? This is a statistical problem. To approach a mathematical simulation we must know the characteristics of the communication system. What channels do we use and how?

We emit electrical fields and organize them in a way that can be picked up, by electrocardiograms, electroencephalograms, and other mechanical extensions of our senses.

We emit heat energy, as anyone who has slept with someone else or been in a crowded room well knows. Photographs may be taken by means of infrared radiation and identify the person who emits. But the emissions of infrared radiation are ordinarily outside of awareness until we move into close range. Some other species orient completely by infrared sense organs. Our own are not as yet explored.

Each person is a reflected-light emitter. The discovery of fire allowed man to control a primary source of light. Man is able to control his reflection of light to some degree by intention. The color of his skin is variable and can be altered by cosmetics. Clothing may be changed to reflect in different zones different bands of light. And the reflected-light emission has a longer range than sound except in fog conditions.

Each person as he clomps through space acts as an emitter of sound. These sound emissions are in large measure unintentional. There is the swishing sound that is running fast, the quick clicking of her footsteps, the sound of his breathing, and many varied and unlanguaged sounds that enable the blind man or the blowpipe Pygmy to create an acoustical identity for each of us. There is the heart beating one can occasionally hear in an excited still room, and those who listen hear the sound of breathed air rushing through the windpipe as a gasp.

All these sounds are in addition to the sounds that we make with the tongue, mouth, and lips, and by the use of the voice box. The latter sounds are in our culture intentional and are to some the only language. The variation in physiological response to human sound emissions, like the calling of a moose to his mate, are yet to be explored. In other species these are highly formalized.

That humans use the high-frequency component of sounds as an orienting tracking signal is extremely likely. The tracking signal emitted from the target but homed in by the seeking system sets an orientation so that one man can find another without looking—as when he comes up from behind. Finding another is a part of communication: losing another breaks down this process, like the heat-seeking missile that has gone beyond its range for perceiving the hot switchback jet engine.

Each of us emits a particular odor, as do all other animals. We become used to our own smell and our own body sounds, so that we lose our awareness, but awareness of another who suddenly enters our smell-emission zone is important. In our culture the intentional reception and emission of smell is carefully bathed out. But children know their family members by their smells. Their smaller stature puts their noses closer to our smell-emitting organs. There may be many other kinds of energy emissions that each of us sends and that untutored children are aware of. If we contact the children's world, they may teach us about their sense before we train it out.

These are concentric circles around the human within which specific signals systems operate. Touch, smell, and the others all have their range and characteristics. Change and the rate of change from that rhythm to which the organism is accustomed shift the behaviors of the message receiver.

The range and characteristics of communication on any particular channel depend upon the physical characteristics of that channel more than is realized. Changes in such weather conditions as wind or rarity and density of air alter the sound system. The sun's intensity for reflection alters the shadow configurations on the face, changing its message-exchange functioning.

We are captured by the exchange medium as well as by limitations which are inherent to our receiving-sending systems. Only a very small percentage of the capacity of our

114

receiving-sending systems is used. Attrition is trained in. As we grow we can simply omit the exchange media irrelevant to the coding system that the culture defines.

In any particular culture, among a particular species, certain information-exchange media are tutored to be enhanced: others are actively diminished. The Eskimo learn to use hearing in a way which allows them to differentiate their field of visual whiteness in a manner quite magical to those of the temperate zone. Each culture specializes in the utilization of a particular range of the information exchange potential available to us. There has been very little effort to train those of one culture in the skills of another. When the skills of another are different they are rarely recognized. An altered expertness in sampling and using a particular range of energy for perception is instead denied by lack of contact. The information source patterning a different system may be unacknowledged or obliterated by disbelief or magical naming. And all opening possibilities that do not match expectation have no way of entering a limited input system.

The family whose input is different may be called sensitive, primitive, or asocial. A freely declared, broadened capacity to take in raw data and to process it into expanding information is not appreciated. But it is just such people who can help us to match our advanced instrumentation with biological advancement, making a technology of survival.

Each person walks through space surrounded by spheres of information sending. Another person crossing through that sphere may be alerted by his scanning that this is not random noise. How he will respond to this information depends upon the state of his own information sending-receiving system with which he tunes in to complete the transmitting-receiving circuit.

In some cultures the visual medium of exchange is most important. In other cultures, two people reaching the proximity at which sound can be exchanged are inclined to give this sound primary significance. In still others it is the smell that counts. In bathing countries this emission is exchangeable only as perfumed by intention or within intimate distances. "She is hot" suggests a radiating distance measured in inches. Body-limb distance is the perimeter of direct touch. And family cultures may be identified by their variation in this signal exchange system.

Much of this information exchange is never translated into words or even thoughts, but remains as a primitive knowledge that may be sensed only when distorted.

Two brothers meet. They exchange glances and grunts—a few social words. And in this exchange a tremendous amount of information has passed. But, if they ask each other what information, neither knows. It is not that the words are particularly informative, but rather the whole sequence of nonintentional behaviors that have become exceedingly familiar. Between each other their shifting and changings are readily decoded into important but unlanguageable information. That this information does not govern the meeting behaviors of daughters-in-law, who are outside the family communication exchange system, is not surprising. This may be nonetheless distressing to those who do not comprehend that they are outside not by reason of exclusion, but by reason of early code learning not shared. And the brothers who do share often have no awareness that the information exchange is not contained in their intentional communication. And this exchange may become boring or frustrating to those looking on who see so little happening.

One of the problems that develops within a family is an undecipherable discordance between the intentional and the unintentional communication ranges. On two different channels they send irrelevant messages without sending on a third—a key for decoding this kind of signal system. In some families the intricate message sending-receiving systems have many different sets relaying different information, and the receiver may be unable to decode this matched message in a way that makes his reply coherent. Such inhabitants of the Tower of Babel may have no awareness of their fragmented voices as heard by an outsider. Those who have experienced this crosstalk learn to filter out the passages that are too broken. They replace full contact with predictions whose congruence with the message sent requires the highest sensitivity. This process is very tiring. Sometimes the family members learn to filter out almost all communications as noise. If this happens very early they may experience sensory deprivation—the silence of a factory so loud and blinding that one cannot find one's neighbor or a decent chance to talk. Children who have experienced extreme lack of contact become like nomads in the desert, talking and repeating to themselves, locked in by a private system.

Sometimes the family has rules for shifting emphasis from one intentional message channel to another.

In some families the message exchange system that is attended is largely intentional. Such a family would be called

intellectual by those who communicate by intense awareness of unintentional physiological message-sending; these
families are called emotional. To this emotional family a
teardrop may be just *one* word.

This division into two common groups leaves out a third
—the families who use the difference between the emotional
and intellectual message as the primary message unit. The
translation problem between a husband and wife who derive
from these different groups may be extreme unless the different languages are brought to awareness.

Within the unintentional communicators, there are those
families who speak mostly with their bodies: pantomime is
the usual means of communication.

In the mouth families, if you watch their mouths you get
the basic information and an emotional context for their
thoughts as verbally reported.

Among the eye families, it is the eyes that are the important signal exchange apparatus, and you must watch each
flick.

There are, as well, the upper-face families and the lower,
each using one part more expressively than the other.

And sometimes major messages are transmitted by hands.
This variation of course is present not only in families, but
is an important variant from one culture to another.

The tone families use variations in tone of voice or in its
volume to set the context for the verbal message. There may
be no verbal message, except a constant repetition of a circular pattern of words, the important message being the tone,
the volume, or the rate and rhythm in which they are
spoken.

Among the prop families, the degree of disarray of their

props and the muscle movement implied can set the context for a verbal exchange that may be similarly more or less meaningfully arranged. And it is the state of the living room plus words that makes the message unit: same words less mess are a different message.

Among the distance families, to-and-fro movements between close and distant set a range which, as it varies, may be a most significant exchange system. A four-foot-distant conversation or a walking conversation may have a meaning entirely different from a four-and-a-half-foot conversation standing still.

Then there are the sequence families in which who approaches whom, or who opens the conversation by approaching within a range that demands conversation, may be more important than what is said.

All of us share all these characteristics to a greater or lesser extent. Cultures are built upon such variations.

A family trains its members to find the usual places and times where a message can best be picked up or filtered out in *its* kind of family. Each person may not be aware that what he experiences is predicated on his own capacity to refine his scanning movements, that is, to direct his sensory intake apparatus to be ready at the point where he predicts the action of his interest will take place.

The kind of exchange experienced will depend upon being trained and learning to correct this prediction by rapidly changing the position of the intake apparatus as new information becomes available. His whole body is like a roving radar homing in on a message. Each movement senses the simultaneous reception and seeking out the signals that hold meaning. This process of contact grows with being alive.

119

Each span in the developmental spiral has its energy transformations that are natural to each moment's age and recollection. And every living creature knows the convergence of what was scarcely felt into a pattern useful to survival. Such points of convergence grow themselves into structures that organize the next seeking. This structuring into patterns governs the decisions as to what will be conceived in awareness. Verbal language structures the units that are common to those who share the language. Language can contain more or less contact.

These namings become scanning devices reinforcing the perception of that which has been named. And the reinforcement to awareness of an aspect of the whole grows into more naming. This labeling-finding-labeling is one growth cycle.

Verbal language is assumed to be a useful representation of a common experience, but sometimes symbols become an end in themselves, unrelated to growth. Then you cannot find a job without experience or experience without a job. Each abstractive system has its own characteristic semantic dilemmas. Each can only label within its particular perspective. When a set of man-made formal semantic rules is unwittingly made absolute, it limits exploration of what was left out by that particular system. And the lack of an informal system or a "meta" system can slow the evolution of language to fit new experience.

The use of intentional symbols to contact reality varies immensely from family to family. In some families, the intentional communication system leads to the development of an image of self—me—that is languaged in a way that makes no contact with the patterned convergence of experiences from within. In some, the language of outer body movement, of inner self, of flesh and environment rarely move together in shared experience. Then words have little meaning, and the whole world is full of cocktail-party talk, which has no consequence for staying alive. Then all that the word "sex" implies is a judgment "to sin with," and the richness of all the world's bathrooms is not shared with one's personal sensations.

If one's idea of himself is not experienced as a naming of what lies within him, if one has not known that others know intimate sensations as well—even those that cannot be worded—then contact and the growing of each other are very difficult to experience. And in such a situation, mental representations, which are a mimicry to fill this void—mere mouthings—prevent contact, and this is a vicious cycle.

In teaching the young child, the parents depend upon the child's capacity to communicate to them what the child experiences as being done to him by them as his teachers. And they depend upon his returning information to know how he is interpreting within his own context and perspective the new experience that is happening. What it would have meant to me if I were he is not enough. This is just a scanning image to search out his response. The parent depends upon the child's capacity to communicate so that the parent can correct and send his own messages in a way that the child can decode as the parent intends.

Some families are expert at encoding their messages so as to make them available for decoding by other family members in the way in which they were intended to be decoded. The message then gets through.

Other families encode their messages without regard for the other person's decoding system. Such messages do not get through as intended. Or, the message received may be derived from the message sent via a decoding process unrelated to the intention of the sender: the placement of stamps on a letter is read as a code to the letter, though the sender was unaware that this would have meaning to the receiver. If he had known that his letter would be interpreted in terms of the stamps, he could have used this channel for message-sending. This lack of knowledge is a common problem in some families, and infuriating to all until they become aware that they are not speaking the same language.

The unintentional act of placing the stamp does tell a story when a common formalized code of words or behavior exists between receiver and sender. A problem arises when one generation's etiquette has no meaning to another's. For if the teenager's encoding process is vintage 1975 and the parents are Victorian, there may be no communication, even though they talk as if they were communicating about immediate and personal issues—like the chores.

Similarly, the stamp story between a husband and wife who follow different codes may be couched in mundane exchanges about seeing a television show or getting the plumbing fixed. The message of no-message-exchange-possible does not get through. Nothing gets done.

When people are unaware that they do not or cannot speak the same language, the messages received are perceived as if congruent with the messages expected to be sent and received, and no one becomes aware that they are out of contact except to have a sense of isolation, which is unexplainable.

The assumption of congruency between message-sent encoding and message-received decoding is always an extreme problem. This problem grows as the unexpected and absurd aspects of the message that can signal incongruence and inaccuracy in the encoding-decoding process are themselves left out. And humor is no longer shared.

As this lack of contact grows it is increasingly maintained by loss of input from the other that could correct and shift the image. Energy is used instead to force the other to become congruent with expectation. The scanning operation has become a self-reflexive mirror feeding back to the sender its own message as if it were response. Such eating one's own tail may result in deprivation.

contact

INFANTS HAND and mother's finger—process contact. Hand trajectory weaving toward finger. Return information. Finger weaving toward hand. Farther apart. Closer. Small hand —index finger playing, both moving through an eyeview. Felt by moving each his own in the field of child and mother's relation. Hand—separate finger: gravitational pull. Eyelids flicker, changing the image, each as trained. And the flow of grasping hand and larger curling finger extend each other in a dance of energy, pattern, concentration, discontinuity, and transformation, warmth, pink, moist, gentled motion.

Each dancing of child and mother returns information of the other's presence as their touch contacts. They grasp firm tight warm imagining accurately even while distant. Contact freshens trajectories alive to each other. Time's flow of action is information weaving the context of finger and hand's exploring touch. And mother and her infant learn each other.

In this field of flowing movement, two lovers—a mother and her child—teach each other to find what they can each experience. And she lets him touch gently by approaching as a mother bird nuzzling new wings from the nest. She plays with the hand, speaking with her fingers as all animals do, and he replies with the movement of his hand—this is contact.

Contact is communication process and information exchanging. How you turn your head to listen governs what voice you hear. Turn your ears toward where you think the sound might be. Predict, expect, tune in. Finding no sound of interest, drop out. Turn the head again, you may find a sound unexpected to the hearing search. Tune in. Predict, play the game of mother's finger and child's full hand. Search for response and define what was expected by what happened next. We all do it.

The intermingled bodies that make and choose the data as relevant to correcting the very next move have a purpose that spirals into happening thoughtlessly. As we move through the time and space of each next step, we dimly know the restricted possibilities for the subsequent next. We are restricted by the position we are in and by the timing sequence of our progression: the frog can only jump to jump to the next near lily pad, and we can only move to the next step. The immediate future has a limited probability, yet it is an open and expanding system, even after the freshening of a family crisis that resolves in surprises.

We cannot go backward into the sameness that existed before. We cannot at present reverse our time direction. Hindsight remains a symbolic statement. The past has only a limited contact with the dialogue-of-now in process. The concept "contact" requires unlearning the clock that gives equal time to past and future but none to now. We make contact more easily when we acknowledge and use the real uncertainty that belongs to the as-it-happens progression-growth time rather than the stationary-point to stationary-point time. Happening-now time is not noon-to-noon time. We have too long thought of life as unknown between landmarks. Life is not a series of still pictures moved infinitely fast to fool our senses.

We need new scientific theory to communicate our experience of the opening present. The old Aristotelian way puts living into equidistantly spaced boxes. Hours are lengths. This linear time does not touch the living fabric. A tulip as it opens—is opening—is not merely the connection of its past and its future, nor is its present beyond measure or conception. Can we discover formal language to make the present explicit? Informally we do this in our nonverbal language. We do compute the growth game, but it is not in our tradition to speak of it as it is happening. Contact is moment-to-moment evolving, in contact with ever-widening context. The moment of now as it expands and contracts maintains change at a manageable level.

A man's time at a cocktail party is variously constructed. Early he corrects his image to the scene. As he procures corrective information he gradually tunes in his scanning apparatus searching through the figures. If he finds a target he homes in. Then he changes his timing. Her lifted eyebrows keep moving him toward his moving target. She may sense his presence. He nears and receives more information. He overhears her conversation. She may be selecting behavior so as to gain impact. He begins the body conversation hoping to call forth in their moment of impact the first acknowledging glance of conversation. If their impact does not grow, they pass by—unknown.

This happens, it is highly structured, it is measurable in practice, but formal language does not encode the familiar.

Common people-happenings have not been studied, they are givens. We know more about the moon than about living contact.

Contact is making music together, growing as a creation of contact between loins that experience each other's rhythms into something new. A new fire building. Is growing. Is contact. Each movement gives awareness of the moving of another in a total field of bedtime movement building fast or slow. And humans live contact with skill, without book knowing. One cannot stop the action to describe it. Time is a contact dimension. The presence of each other over time evolves the system's change. One knows by living contact, and well-timed grunts are its most eloquent description. And these changes mix the old ingredients into a new form that can hold new ingredients—and two adults so entwined create their child.

They move through time astride the rolling hands of the clock timed by the style that organizes them into a living unit. One night has not the same duration as the next. And their lively way of growing changes what there is for them to experience. Some experiences are quite beyond their expecting, and often these are most enriching. Familiar is a family word.

Some family styles grow familiar discovery. This is their style. How can they make a style of searching out what none knew to exist? They value the unexpected they bump into. When what had no existence in expectation is met as an experience, its information is picked up like a bump on the head or a bruise, it may be felt with the hand-grasped shoulder long before it is spoken, and family ears and eyes and head may turn to a newness.

Two sending and receiving stations contacting each other are more than a wire between two terminals. Living things cannot be simplified by describing anatomy alone. An arm moved with its shoulder held by another is not an anatomical problem. But the messages are there in the way they grow their holdings. A family is not its home, or its income, or its conversation. Labeling ingredients or goals or measuring these on psychological tests does not catch the local swirling, nor the capacity for growing.

There are those who conceive of *their* world as being a limit of that which exists. They lose the matrix out of which they are selecting. They do not enjoy the flow of loins beyond their knowing. And human senses make available ranges of sensations, flows, and patterns different from those of other species with different kinds of sensing systems, inner clocks, and means of orientation. The range of sensations that humans can literally encompass is limited, but the capacity to meet experience is unpredictable.

I cannot understand the living present by studying its context of the past. Like infant growings: standing upright is at first a newness unrelated to the experience of others who have stood before. I seek to induce you into sensing the new forward questions. We seek words for involving formal thinking with forward motion in progress. We acknowledge the irreversibility of time. The standing child plonks softly to the ground, each time newly wedded. Our living, unlike our symbols, cannot be reversed. Formal rules that deny this reality are out of contact.

And this way of thinking, building forward with the present in its focus, catches in its net the growth of a child as he reaches forward into structuring what never existed for him. This way of thinking allows us to contact learning as being alive.

The primitive drum of one family's way of life catches its members' every muscle fiber into aliveness. But one family's use of timing is different from another's. Some families time their presentation of new experiences to each other—their bumping into unexpected behaviors—so that they will grow the whole to be in contact with each member; others, though seemingly providing the same information, do so when there is no family way of hearing. Timing is the control language of change.

Past-time description has been our convention for setting the present happening in perspective: the family uses its recollected past to control the meaning of the present. But as with each course at a banquet, the taste of the last course is changed as a new taste unfolds. Past and present evolve each other. The family's use of the ongoing present also determines what will be recollected and its meaning. The dessert changes the memory of the meat by changing its context. This changing of the past returns to alter the present as it is conceived in terms of the past: the memory of the meat is changed by dessert, but as this memory of the meat changes, so the dessert tastes different in contrast. The old ways of simplifying cannot encompass this significant way of evolving reality, and each family has its own style of managing this timing language.

Though this evolution spirals confortably through relativism's time, this spiraling seems complex to those who think of their lives as a straight line. Those families who respect such linear logic grow a distortion that loses them their contact. And, though this appears abstract, the informal language which makes sense of what cannot be stated in easy English is the most important teaching of the family. It is the earliest behavior of the family that styles a geometry of space-time to the child's own way of learning.

The basic structural notions, as informally taught in each family's moment-to-moment style, vary widely from culture to culture, east to west, family to family. And ordinary words have different meanings.

The images created in these lines model many living systems. The concept of explosion—of multiplication like the rhythm of our cells as they grow, wax, and wane—provides a structural map that contacts the growing seasons of a family's life. In describing the living of a family, linear conceptions are highly artificial. The living ebb and flow of a family's behavior circulate even as it expands to include experiences beyond the expectations that its language encompasses. The family language of nods and timings is many times richer than our present technical language can measure. In our Western formulations, both number and literary language are wedded to a cause-effect, subject-predicate grammar. That a child is the result of his parents' training, that the individuals in a family are responsible for the family unit—these are fallacies that are considered simple truths. Living behavior is not that way. Our capacity to apprehend the requirements for survival is diminished by the attempt in some families and among social scientists to love linear logical sequences and to conceptualize themselves as inorganic.

The human creature, like every species to date, has pretended that the world is limited by his own particular prohibitions. Until we can compare our social life with that of other intelligent species, we shall continue to be unaware of the techniques of contact natural to humans. The study of families gives a start in this direction.

As family members walk into my office, the most important assessment that I feel it necessary to make is the amount of contact they experience with one another. A father sits quietly, interested in what his family is discussing. He sends no signals that are received by the other family members, and he receives no response information. No one knows he is listening, no one contacts him. His unheard signal-sending, his interest, and his conclusions are uncorrected, and his ability to communicate with them decays further. He is increasingly silent to them. His presence is not experienced by the others in a manner that allows them to feel an impact other than the image of his silence. They fill in with an unreal image of a man who is disapproving. Fill-in images, uncorrected by return, extinguish awareness of this absence of contact. They think they know him. The family members fill in with worn-out stereotypes—with uncorrectable abstractions. They may use the past to avoid and manage the present.

To be in contact with oneself is to be aware that so much is unlanguageable. Contact requires omitting information. Privacy is necessary: there is no way to tell oneself all about oneself. We can meaningfully language into worded thoughts only what we believe others are ready to hear. From this we stretch a little. New ideas that do not find a place of impact soon die. Some families are more expert at thinking with more primitive symbols than words. Feelings, we call them.

It is useful to differentiate between privacy of feeling, unlanguageable feeling, solitude, and no contact. Solitude and privacy tend to be by choice. No contact is not only the incapacity to hit the target, it is also being unaware of those messages from the world of other persons and phenomena that make awareness possible.

The word "imagination" has to do with ability to use for discovery the expectant images one has created by prejudgment. A capacity to shift the prejudged expectation, the search image, can liberate new perspectives. Learning such flexible contact with one's own intuition allows bumping into more new data at the edge of one's conservative, more logical expectations. Unexpected happenings can form themselves into new search images and new perspectives. The new perspective is tested against what actually occurs as seen when it stands in this perspective. The search image is continuously refined by trial and error, and this spiraling capacity to make and use new contact is called creativity. When I see a family in my office, this creativity is what I look for first. It is the family function that provides me with the most basic awareness.

Three members of the family are seated together. If one's leaving does not influence the remainder, then the two left are simply the subtraction of one from three. This is a linear situation where arithmetic concepts work—but this is not a creative family. If one's leaving doubles the influence of the second and trebles the influence of the third, the situation may still be dealt with as a noncontact family. In a contact family, the father's leaving so changes the mother and child's relationship that they no longer exist as just the remaining part of the whole. The operations of the contact family are nonlinear. What they create does not solely depend on what they receive or what mixture of ingredients is present among them. They live (grow) the phenomena they create by their contact. This simple fact, well known to any social person who values the novelty of experiencing contact, means that behavior cannot be predicted by summing or subtracting or dividing or multiplying family-member styles.

The meanings of each family member are inextricably tied together with the whole. The contact family is one and many organisms, all evolving each other, and each evaluating changes what is to be evaluated, even as it is happening.

Those who have worked with families are astonished to observe that husband and wife when seen without their children are intrinsically different people than when seen with them. One does not expect so much difference. It is as if they were not the same people. An expert hostess knows that one grouping of guests will bring out qualities in each guest that may be entirely hidden in another grouping. Personnel managers and executives depend upon their capacity to arrange groupings that will get more work done.

People inflame each other in such different ways. In different numbers and places they are literally not the same people. Those fired by the action they created may no longer be the people they were. Each person responds to the responses of each other as this alters the event.

A wife at the store may operate on her cart-pushing husband quite differently from a wife in her kitchen. A husband at work may be strong and effective while at home his stature and decision power sink. If we are defining this husband in terms of his weight in pound units as compared with a national average, he is not seriously altered as he moves from office to home. If we are defining weight in terms of his effectiveness, the husband has changed remarkably.

134

The family's contact with the outside world may be such that it will prepare its offspring families for the shifting experience of a coming generation. Contact implies the capacity to maintain constancy by changing.

The rapidly increasing rate of change means changing the rate at which we shift the family to meet new developments. Without contact, old behavior repeated becomes useless and obsolete. Standing still does not exist. Some families do not change according to the subtle changes implicit, for example, in change of neighborhood. A shift in sidewalk of a new home means changing one's step, but not to some. And the children may respond to the new neighborhood as if it had no connection with the old. They are unable to change their pattern so that the matching of themselves with the new neighbors is not so unlike the results of the previous matching. The fresh start does not necessarily evolve skill in evolving. Both continuous and discontinuous change is necessary to hold the base of constancy necessary for communication. Consistency is not sameness. Some people save up change and periodically blow out their old ways. Some feel joyful and others depressed in the process. There are many styles of contact.

sickening intensities

AN EXTREMELY out-of-contact family may have become trained over several generations into seeking the kinds of marriages that generate a style of life that does not require depth of skill in learning. This family cannot sweep the horizon to take in the wide range of unexpected data. This family is out of contact because it is only minimally informed. Its stability is built on sameness. It may try to fill the gap with elaborate message sendings and theories about communication, but it can produce only crude, thin forms of information exchange. And this has nothing to do with being primitive. A primitive system may be luxuriant.

Loss of skill in expressing or in listening can slow the growth of the spiral of information exchange that links people in a growing loop of communicative action. It is in the mapping of unknowns that humans excel, even as they use what was ambiguous to grow the next level of more relevant ambiguity.

Men are different from women and both are different from children. Each is ambiguous to the others in ways that extend far beyond that which is presently appreciated, and some of this grows from differences as yet as untranslatable as the coding of different species.

But from this broader field of being, which is unshareable, each family member has certain trickling stimulus streams, which, as they wander about and sometimes join, become available for contact and reception by other family members. And the very closeness of a family trained together allows this joined skill in knowing what cannot be said. Where contact is possible, fields of information concentrate and form into junctures out of which a network of family contact is built. Each family member has streams of interest and experience that no other family member could conceivably contact. Yet a simple "Hello" from a brother, who is of the same inheritance, may speak a breadth of knowing that may remain out of awareness yet be available to influence decisions.

And some families determine their members' privacy with or without any awareness of how much is already private by being untranslatable. What is untranslatable may be denied by everyone talking of togetherness as if that meant there was nothing unshared or unshareable. The brothers do not make contact while speaking of this joining.

In some families each member attempts to capture even those stimulus bonds which are in no way contactable. No behavior is accepted as beyond explanation or naming by the family. And the family members are taught by the family that no existence is allowed any one of them that all cannot know or understand. Some families teach that what is not shared by all is attack.

But contact is not increased by capturing all channels so as to make them converge into meaning. Convergence is a happening. The contact process is subverted if the evaluation and discussion of contact become the major message. Becoming aware of unexpected divergences, of variation, can be a signal that one hasn't sent the message in a way that makes it understood as one had intended. Or it can be a signal for a newness that is far more important to explore than the message of one's original intention. The filigree of choice—when to explore or when to correct—holds a music that within a common family's style sings differently for each person's style. To some, divergence is always a signal that sets off anger and depression. There are those who can explain everything; they kill off the noisy freshening provided by an unexpected smile.

Some families capture communication machinery by attending the way messages occur as if the way were the message. Their problem increases when there develops over time an awareness that the family relationship is increasingly limited: then message sending and receiving become a fight between communication companies, each saying "Let's communicate" or "You don't tell me anymore." What anyone says has no simple meaning. It is how much was said to whom that is now the message. When what one says bears no resemblance to what is heard, actual silence is more communicative than "as-if communication," as many silent-at-home family members know.

When communication systems are totally captured by the family, they become very special and ingrown. The children may be experienced early within this system to believe that the novelty that is not obtainable within their family does not exist. They learn to live in a low-novelty environment perpetuating the family style.

A peculiar kind of contact may suit the marriage of two

out-of-contacts who, meeting, share the few points of contact they retain. This kind of marriage may or may not experience a child (or all of them) into believing that what exists is limited to his family's limited contact techniques. Some children react to extreme lack of contact within their family by learning to avoid this way of life. They value contact, they avoid their parents. They learn within the freedom that luck creates—a family friend, an uncle or aunt, may provide the resources. The lucky child of a noncontact family may build a family of nonhuman experience—trees and rafts and swimming holes shared with friends his own age. This child is raised by his contemporaries and their reflections of their families. This freedom may produce in the next generation an unfettered marriage that creates beyond the limits of its epoch . . . or it may not. The freedom may be best obtained with lots of friends around. A poorly chosen mate or one accepted by and bound to his family can make this freedom only periodic—when the boys are around.

Special out-of-contact systems can grow children with a more narrow sense of self than has previously developed in such a family. The child who does not escape may join a family whose obsolescence is made more acute by the real world's forward movement. Having from birth learned from the example of his parents' relationship the techniques for maintaining out-of-contact isolation, he may be even more empty of contact experience than either of his parents.

But another sibling, a younger brother, who arrives and has his older brother or sister to help may not become so caught in the parents' marriage. He may be catalyzed by his brother's behavior into being able to discover each parent separately. He learns a more vital way of living.

For the child who is caught, functional utility and detail

of information are trained out of experience by a wordy moralism, called worldly, which the parents use to avoid contact with each other. Word permutations and combinations replace contact. There is a prejudicial restriction of the scanning of the field. The child of this family is walked by the family style through a world carefully selected for his need. His parents may be restricted only when in the family presence of each other. But for the child who chooses to live within this presence there are out-of-contact tricks to be learned. If he joins in faking broadened experience by becoming a verbal expert at argumentation, attack, and defense, or if he uses his senses to select information that will allow him to ward off the fear of disaster, then this fear may use up his energy so that he cannot learn to cope with the actual stream of events. Observation and learning may be replaced by a limited form of intuition that does not allow unintentional correction of intuitive error as necessary for contact. Such intuition undervalues, for example, the rough man's capacity to be gentle when moved by another's warmth. Such intuition can become grossly deceptive. Intuition must be frequently tested by contact if it is to be predictively trusted.

A slight feint and quick response returned may serve as correction to the intuitive system, particularly when it seemed a needless movement. A testing by pressing what seems absurd, only a joke, may be the crucial test. It is in high ambiguity moments that the richest information evolves. The skillful use of rapid automatic intuitive process grows as each testing facilitates the next. Such learning to learn occurs in the family school just as do the noncontact lessons.

Some families learn their intuitive lessons without lightness, humor, or perspective. There is no play. The cost of building major crises when the testing has become too profound a commitment may be so high that it is a disastrous investment. Intuition corrected by bloodletting is not the intuition of those who have been allowed to pursue the easy contact learning natural to children.

The prejudging expectation of some families filters their possible reservoir of intuitively processed information down to a limited awareness. Intuition is neither trusted nor tested. The problem here is maintaining contact with themselves. Contact is reduced whenever holding to symbolic reasonableness prevents using the natural reservoirs that exist to enrich the family pool. A logical husband can kill a wife's intuition so that she gets depressed.

Either intuitive preference or intentional reasonableness or both may be selectively tapped to make "data" available to fill in for lack of contact. The "data" are used to prevent those ambiguous moments when return corrective information breaks preoccupation with knowing one is right or wrong. It is the flow of uncertain moments among the information islands that makes the system grow. In these families where ambiguity is avoided, a ritual is prescribed and is intuitively sensed as being comfortable, regardless. Then the family's reality is like a dream kept true.

The dream is limiting: Christmas is practiced with exactness. Theirs is the only possibly correct Christmas that exists. As time and circumstance can be more completely controlled, this kind of family is more logically able to maintain its inflexible stability. The errant family member's freedom is a threat. He is called delinquent.

The brother who is not caught may be able to dismiss the

behavior of his parents together as a kind of absurdness with which he does not care to deal. The sister may help her cousin to influence her brother toward withdrawing from the family and making contact with other school friends. The older brother and sister may be caught themselves.

The remaining family has its truth—a fabricated reasonableness that is closed and logical, more logical than reality could be.

These who are used to arguing know that it is possible to build a reasonableness to prove any preconception. It is increasingly easy to do so as data are reduced to selective abstraction. It is especially possible to lie retrospectively. No one remembers all the details, and the story line can be variously structured. And the younger brother who stays away from the family style is labeled "the sick one." In justifying its story, such a family mixes data collected at different times in different circumstances into a supercoherent story showing a reasonableness that is bizarre to the observer once he realizes the family system. Any family so unambiguous, so reasonable, must be crazy—that is the feeling. If he knows only the brother called delinquent, the observer, no matter how skilled he is, will be misled. When the whole family is observed together in an interactive situation, the observer too will be considered bizarre and delinquent by the family. Observers have in the past avoided this situation.

Maintenance of a restricted reasonableness by selective inattention is often not apparent: the family must be viewed in terms of what they leave out of their exchange. Much of what is scientific in its logic is irrelevant. Finding the omissions requires enormous creativity on the part of the observer. The family stifles all those who come in its range by

143

making noncongruent logic seem absurd. Creativity is absent within the factual family system. The "delinquent" brother's newness can be ridiculed as being only a personal presumption and then dismissed. The delinquent brother too will feel absurd in the context of his family even amid their "warmth." The therapist finds that with the younger brother and older brother and whole family present, he is more able to restore contact.

The family is out of contact. The web of self-deceit is so finely silken it does not even shimmer. Shadows cast by the family member who does not fit can reveal the web.

When a family is out of contact, it may actively use such contact as it has to prevent those with real contact skills from unsettling the system. In such a family, what contact skill exists is primarily directed toward denying the intrusion of that which has no place in expectation; it is used to grow increasing formularization. In the extreme, each part of the family works together with the others at preventing anyone from meeting anything or giving out news that would rock their boat. Society at large is kept out. Everything is simplified into a closed ritual. This balancing necessarily grows, each one signaling his next movement so that it can be accurately anticipated intuitively or intentionally. This active preoccupation keeps the boat in port, and the "delinquent" brother, even when he stays with friends, rocks the boat.

Anyone approaching this family is sucked into its formula and finds himself immobilized in a role of expectation unrelated to his own sense of contact. The outsider contacting the family wonders if he is becoming psychotic. This family provides the reservoir out of which psychosis properly nourished may grow.

This whole family apportions its vitality and energy into a series of roles, usually the sides of a conflict that set the casting of the marriage. Over time, each person in the family becomes bound to his roles: he finds no other position in this family. Like an adult at a teen-ager's party, just being not-another-teen-ager is more significant than what kind of adult he is. At such a party each not-a-teen-ager may be formularized as an alien, and regardless of behavior, be experienced as a policeman, rarely as an ally. Working to break out of one role set can build the opposite role. The adult who plays teen-ager may be in for a shock. The strong become the weak and the weak become the strong, for in the family play it is easier to exchange roles. Breaking into contact is very difficult once a family has begun to live without contact.

In the formula families being described, one can name the family members as if they were in a TV soap opera. There are the goodies and the baddies, the lovers, the unrequited, the full and the lonely, the reformers and the ones to be reformed. They act out the same script over and over with only slight variations. What a contrast to the freshness, lightness, and humorous growing in more contactable families.

Sometimes, the formula family is one that combines reduced contact at the input level with *intense relationship*. This apparent paradox can be understood best if each single person is considered to contain within himself all the conflicts that are being enacted in the family drama. Each such person factually keeps his personal dream true by selecting a partner and developing a family that lives out the formula

145

of bad dreams he needs to exist. The family organism works toward reenacting what might in someone else be a dream. The bad dream may simply reconstitute the limited reality with which the person was trained to cope in his childhood family. You will want to avoid such people, but we are all this way to some degree.

To the observer, this kind of narcissistic family-without-contact seems to have an "as if" quality. The ambiguous and uncertain language of becoming cannot stand strongly amid the argumentative firmness of deciding accurately what was. Their logic is exact. Their sense of relevance is peculiar—it admits only what will fit the logical expectation. The inter-loper exposed to this energy field can respond with a sense of disorientation or depression, his own system seems so loose and vulnerable in comparison. Often one member of this family, perhaps the older brother, unable to find contact out-side the family boundaries, succumbs to the absence of con-tact in the presence of so much intense pseudocertainty. This is likely to happen at a time when he becomes aware, even for a short moment, of what he is missing. In despair, he turns from the formula he knows, and seeks contact with the living self within himself.

But this long-irrelevant self inside may be so untrained, so unprotected and primitively separated from the structure of the family formula that, when it breaks through, it is crazy.

Finding contact with one's innards is not easy when one has been trained to live out of contact.

The search for contact reveals poorly tested innards. There glimmers the realization that one must use underde-veloped means of handling powerful primitive feelings. And all of this mixes with the fragments of the out-of-contact

146

shell one had learned to be. And this family-accepted role remains to ridicule the childlike strength's emergence and the power of adult feelings . . . and a hospital may be required to help lend the kind of controlled integration that was never learned. This kind of decompensation in an effort to restore life to what was dead is one form of schizophrenia. The same process happens for most of us day by day as we discover ourselves and our families. And some days bring us more insight than others.

Sometimes the out-of-contact behavior that forms the core of an intensely "close" but empty family is covered up by an altered or special use of formal emotion out of contact with feelings. The child is fed out of a contactless breast, a paper breast, the mother out of an empty husband, and the husband out of a meaningless family. Within the family, the members share dreams that they are receiving kindness, care, love, and affection with extreme sacrifice. But what is being given is unrelated to need: there is no contact between the need, the giver, and the receiver. A high level of faked-up emotion is the family style. In the midst of such an emotional mockery, unheard human basic needs go unmet. Each slight closeness makes the loneliness more extreme. Contact with self and with others is subverted, testing of real feelings is denied, skills in corrective contact operations are unknown. There are so many feelings so intense, but with such fictitious fill-in that they do not satisfy the needs; the search for satisfaction is so consuming that there is no way to play. There is no ambiguity or uncertainty acknowledged when in truth the whole world seems adrift. There is no way slowly to engage an emergent emotion with a course of action that has evolutionary stability. "Emotion" is its name. "He is in love with love" is the common expression. All the performed (or preformed) feeling receives and gives nothing. This intense family life is out of contact, as are all the family members with each other. Decompensation in a member of this kind of family can become one form of psychotic depression. Sometimes death by suicide seems the only way to get a real feeling or to break out of the locked-in system. Only the dream world can provide such certainty that there is no unexpected recontexting possible to relieve the ongoing pain.

The misuse of reality, the distortion of emotion, may be covered by hyperattention to responses from others without awareness that one's own bahavior has limited the probable responses. His statement, "They are all talking about me, even strangers," is kept unrelated to his dark glasses and mufflered face in the middle of the summer (the intention is to hide). In his family, a cough which leaves a formula word unsaid is interpreted as disagreement or attack. When a cough is interpreted as attack on the ward of a psychiatric hospital, as it reasonably was at home, "He's out of contact," they say. When the response of others is not comprehended as a function of one's own signal sendings, the field of contact is dramatically reduced, and behavior becomes oversimplified in its explainability. When unexpected experience is not valued as corrective information or as an invitation to adventure, but is seen only as misunderstanding or attack, there develops a self-verifying mythology. In the extreme, unorganizeable novelty is seen as a destructive force sent by the devil. Desperate needs to defend the family script seen by someone outside the dream world, rather than from within the family context which had made it reasonable, may be called paranoid delusion. This out-of-contact behavior provides ways of disguising the difficulty and need to return to contact with a poorly tested and socially unprogrammed part of self. The fear expressed in concreteness that denies ambiguity is taught by a family style. The family succeeds in living a closeted existence for several generations by careful choice of marriage partners until freed by disruption of the shell.

In the psychotic out-of-control process, the lack of contact is covered by distortion. One form of this cover is intense relating to oneself as seen mirrored in the action of another. Family members are aware of their own deficiencies or strengths only as perceived in another person's behavior. What would be neurotically a conflict within self is lived as a "family drama." The intensity of relationship necessary for such severe disorders to develop grows in a family where husband and wife chose their partners to put outside their own internal conflict learned in their families-of-birth. And this process can pass out-of-contact behaviors over several generations before there is severe disruptions by "illness" or "recovery."

In some families, there has never been contact, and this is *not* covered by such distortion as that noted above. In this kind of family, each person could find other relationships outside the family unit. There are many forms of acceptable divorce which can reconstitute contact for any family member.

But heredity and circumstance together amplify the out-of-contact way of life to intensity which prevents divorce and requires distortion. Both behavioral inheritance and genetic inheritance, matched in succeeding generations with out-of-contact marriages, evolve a reservoir from which psychosis may emerge. In earlier generations, the out-of-contact way of life may work so that there is no apparent disorder. If the out-of-contact style is sustained with great moral distortion, where the family has a very strict moral code and uses it to deny personal crime and violence perpetrated on each other or only on friends, we have another revulsive situation. Then some of the children's children, in order to escape a dead morality, abandon contact with the hated social codes, because they were used to hiding the absence of contact in their family. It is the socializing force of in-contact relationship that allows the family to build in and perpetuate the changing codes of culture and community that maintain identity within change. Breakdown in the empty family that leans on a moral formula for pseudocontact may lead to asocial behavior and to the empty people some label as severe delinquents and social psychopaths.

It is more difficult to construct the problems that are intrinsic to out-of-contact operations covered and maintained by high levels of contention. These are socially more acceptable, but they can be equally problematic as they eat up social energy by continuing to chew at some old rage, once a flag for a vital cause. And some families live out a perpetual hate directed against a socially controversial issue or minority which is never contacted except as filtered through the most extreme prejudgment. And this is sometimes a family way of life that allows an internal dream to appear as if outside. And if the behavior of such a family group is well nourished by a hellish situation, such a family can provide leadership for lynchings.

But too much awareness of the outside world may set a relative contrast, which again makes for an out-of-contact family way of life. It is expressed as difficulty in finding contact with self. The self is reduced by the capacity to receive too much unselected information from the prodigious environment. Lack of contact with self leaves no adequate search image to use in filtering out what is for that moment extraneous contact. There is extreme personal diffusion. This is another circle. A personal radar system always set at high input sensitivity gives a detail of resolution which amplifies awareness of other people's problems. This can build a sense of flowing entirely in the other people's guts in a way that prevents concerted action, or even a minimally focused existence. This kind of diffusion is most evident when decisions must be made, and there is terror that the other person or situation will change its mind. This kind of diffusion has many names. It is most commonly felt by the teen-agers of a family. A need to be organized by strong outside force and a fear of ambiguity provide queer religious or military followers.

Too much amplification on the corrective circuits may also lose the goal. Contact includes accurately selecting the amount of insulation necessary to find simplicity. The people plagued with a nonvariable sensitivity unmatched to the strengths of the signals coming in may have great difficulty in separating intentional and unintentional communication. To this kind of family, a child's unintentional hunger for affection, well defended by intense isolation, becomes the same as the warmth of a lad who *is* warm and able to enjoy affection. For this family, relationships may take fire too soon, rise to high intensity, then as suddenly go out.

There is a sadness in some families that need not have happened had not a very special circumstance been born into

151

their out-of-contact way. They are out of contact in a way that might well be reduced by a next round of children's growing up and marrying so as not to carry on the behavioral inheritance. For this family there is escape in emotional divorce: personal lives outside the family that make the family tolerable. But genetic inheritance changes the flow: a child is born to the family who requires more than the usual contact. This is a child who is more different, more endowed with special genius or more deprived of ability, sensory or motor. Either way, in order to be socialized into a way of being that allows common language to develop, the child needs special understanding in the family. It is not intellectual understanding, but the ability of parents and brothers and sisters and through them the babysitters and nurses and all, to have a contact image of the child's special way of experiencing with the kind of genius or loss that he has. The mother who smiles gently and warmly at her blind child across the room is out of contact if within herself she does not have an image of her child as being unable to see her smile. And I have seen parents of blind children point to an object with their finger, and be furious when the child did not respond. Unwittingly they did not give a sound signal as well that the child would perceive. Families in contact have an image inside of the individual real child which they change as he grows. Members of the out-of-contact family use their idealized image of their own childhood, not as a guide, but as a style of a literal reality. The child exists as a little replica. And this doesn't work if the child happens to be a genius type of child with special skills. He can perceive more detail, needs a richer surround of information, needs a kind of support that acknowledges that he is different.

Such a family can unintentionally bring their genius child up in a closet, closed from the kind of playful learning that would give his difference meaning and a way of being used. If he is sufficiently different he may develop his own style of organizing the world, an idiosyncratic style that spirals his difference into more difference, and evokes the epithets of stupid, or feebleminded, or autistic, or schizophrenic. The out-of-contact family relates to the now-idealized label, making its expectations come true.

Many children's skill in learning, their genius, is blocked by the extreme isolation of the family school or other schools from its evolutionary potential. This kind of loss of contact is costly. Even though one understands the myriads of pathways for each new unfolding moment, one knows that growing up out of contact can mean passing through periods of learning readiness without the child's openness being known by others who make contact. And the system closes. Evolutionary death may come early by exclusion as one clings to the sameness of the past. This process occurs in many variations in all families, cultures, and epochs. And the need for sameness is being changed by our increasing skill at evolving contact. If we can language the process of contact, we can allow our children to evolve in their variations more freely. An evolutionary point of view frees them—and us—to know more profoundly the common body of knowledge and truths being metabolized by our common evolution. We need our children to know us and our ways so that they can teach us their natural contact skills.

a family
and
its people

How does a family catch its people? I do not believe that "a family" equals "its people." You the reader know that you too have been trapped—once as a child and once when the family within you, grown of your expectation, joined with her expectation to form a family that coupled you together into performing its next generation.

Nor do I deny my belief in individual reality. Everyone believes in it.

But who believes that family wars capture their participants? Everyone knows that this happens, no one says it—instead, we look for the cause in components. But, as I have told you again and again each individual, each family member, is caught by family tradition—is swayed and is jumbled and rocked into forgetting that he may not fit a role that is, for the family, right. Then in a moment outside the magnetic inducement, he makes contact, and a decision unfolds. Contact is knowing the reality of the manifold roles and positions and vacant places that squeeze you into shape. A kiss is more than the sum of four lips.

Why not be squeezed if the pressure is right to make you progress—or grow—or explore—or if it is delicious and tender? But contact is knowing that surrender or battle is a choice to be made. Battle has no advantage for all time, nor does meaning. Sometimes, meaningless fighting or loving makes the next action a choice that has meaning. Contact implies that decisions are—sometimes—made not as a token of future direction but just as a testing to reveal what exists. A family may take a course that will drive it onto a springboard that propels it into unknowns that will reveal its implicit structure. In the past, the members could only sense their family, and now they create by pushing down on a spring tightened for recoil and set to be sprung. The family may exaggerate misery until it recoils into contact. The way the trigger is pulled does not create the target, but the timing of a family's trigger-pulling may specify an innocent date into a daughter-in-law. A family catches its people by being so available as a target to so many triggerings. It is an ever-present bull's-eye that explodes energy from many sources—some internal, but others quite unrelated to the kind of timeless explaining that makes the world neat—on paper. The same action a moment later may have an entirely different effect.

A family is a living process that transcends its generations and its people. It moves from Denver to Detroit in a style of training children that relives the grandparents' way. A way of communication does not die when one person is buried. This movement forward into birth and death cannot be contained in descriptions that do not catch the moments of mother, father, and infant being unknowingly cuddled by the family's old way of evolving each other. There is a pattern to this way of behavioral evolution: this growth edge of change can be described.

Can you catch the rhythm of your own participation in your family's dance?

Can you vary the dance by contacting the moment when a slight variation will pull the dance along with you into a counterpoint, freshened by each other's knowing that a change is in progress?

This is the contact you need to know.

You can feel the process when you are aware that there is a pattern and a lawfulness to the way of becoming.

You know the dance of becoming and the dance of obsolescence. You can know it by pulling back or being funny when all the world has never expected that anyone can be absurd—and absurdity is part of becoming. For what seems absurd is often the beginning of change or one wouldn't have known that the move was there to be made.

But I am not speaking in favor of being absurd. I am talking of how one becomes aware of the implicit.

A family's life is largely implicit. It lives far beyond the words that we know. But who needs to know all the perceptions that guide automatic behavior. We need to know only when the patterns of family drunk up with the milk and the toast and the butter of family presence leave us unable to cope with the need to explore and find a way out of a dilemma to which all solutions are bad—miserable—awful—choices. Yes, contact is not making old choices. It is being able to experience the reality of multiple realities, each real from a particular point of view.

And contact is knowing that one can be captured by the point of view of the system in which you are living. To play the system, once you have revealed it to yourself, so that you speak your wishes by actions that produce change even as they are misinterpreted (in the way that you calculated) is a part of the art of contact.

Knowing the synchrony of irrational excitement that will balloon into crisis and then into guilty despair allows you to decide when your action will be meaningful communication —and perhaps even helpful.

Knowing when the family system is locked against change enables one to seek during the locked-in time those activities which are better pursued when family novelty is low and conformity of all the family members to a foregone conclusion is inevitable.

I have made it my business to watch the personalities of families unfold. I have watched all the family members' relief when a family tradition that had captured every single member was finally revealed—for it had always been implicit. Then one family member, who was in contact with the reality of the family organism's few open moments, made just one simple move that forced everyone to resist to such an extent that everyone was aware that they had been captured. Then he made a joke, which brought tears to their hearts, for the family members all knew that for too long they had each been captured. And not much was said because there was no reason for discussion.

And sometimes everyone is sad that their lives are so somber and their fun is middle-aged. They are afraid to be younger. The risk is too great.

How often each person's being boxed into repetitious disenchantment is no one's fault, but finding fault is a way of saying something when contact is lost. Touching becomes a cruel slap and a gut-pulling that prevents the empty feeling and the knowledge that living is going down the drain. And this happens more often as families protect themselves from death by retracting those tentacles which gave them a life outside the family and provided the perspective of moments of distance. Such moments allow the kind of expert behavior that blows the whole family out of its doldrums.

Sometimes joining the cycling process and driving it beyond the point where it can return to its usual oscillation is enough to destroy the circular trap. Escalating the absurdity of what seems a maladaptive repetition may reveal that it is adaptive—to a circumstance that you were not at all aware of. In a family where the belly punch is reduced to just a sick feeling and a quick recovery, it is difficult to punch so hard that there can be no recovery. But what seems an almost killing blow can reveal repetition, and a decision is made. It is hard to give affection when attack is the cover for extreme isolation. But these ways of being actively real are possible when you see beyond sticky moments and glue drowning the dying marriage while morally saving it from illicit acts of freshening rejuvenation or separation. When a family is caught good, getting untrapped is morally wrong. The family glue may drown children as well as their parents.

Children break out by behavior that the family, including themselves, considers meaningless. When adolescence comes, this is the time of knowing the absurdity of both adults and adolescents. It is a time of breadth of vision—often disappointing. It is a time of escape from the last generation's restrictions. Following through adolescent insight without dampening its vigor is harder when the family's tradition is liberal, but stuck in the old style. Following one's own integrity when one also accepts the strength of a family's joined integrity requires accepting the ambiguity of change whose control rests outside as well as among its family members. For in a family, each person's change means that everyone must shift. And no member of any family controls, or can predict, what the ingredients of change will produce.

Each family does have a style of becoming and of evolving and of maintaining its equilibrium within the changings. The logic of becoming has a discipline that will be made clear as our science begins to specify change producing change in all the elements engaged in the reaction, including the observer. This revolution in science is near. It is overdue. It is vital to surviving.

There is a richness in the family and in all systems where information flows in the way I have described. A child is taught by multitudinous touchings with family members— by all the touchings with smell and muscles and smiles that he meets and that change his touchings. And the whole world of growing things is entwined in these loops. It is the beauty of growing change that the same ingredients mixed in the same ways with the slightest well-timed variation produces surprise. Each newborn is a renaissance of possibilities constrained only by the pace of an evolution that denies meaning to too much change. Thus the species preserves just the amount of sameness that makes reliable communication possible. Too much change creates a gap that cannot be bridged. We are straining to render technical, and teachable, the successful ways of managing the gap as it is widened now by our rapid unlearning of obsolescent styles of existence.